PATHWAYS
TO THE
SPIRIT

100 WAYS TO BRING THE SACRED INTO DAILY LIFE

✡

SUSAN SANTUCCI

MJF BOOKS
NEW YORK

Published by MJF Books
Fine Communications
322 Eighth Avenue
New York, NY 10001

Pathways to the Spirit
LC Control Number 2006938833
ISBN-13: 978-1-56731-837-1
ISBN-10: 1-56731-837-1

Design by Claudyne Bianco Bedell

This edition published by MJF Books in arrangement with Hyperion, an imprint of Buena Vista Books, Inc.

Printed in the United States of America.

MJF Books and the MJF colophon are trademarks of Fine Creative Media, Inc.

MV 10 9 8 7 6 5 4 3 2 1

For Michael and Justine

ACKNOWLEDGMENTS

My sincerest thanks to Ehrick Wright, Amanda Sobel, Eric and Elizabeth Carlson, and Beth Greenberg for their valuable feedback and encouragement through all stages of this manuscript. I am fortunate to have such wonderful and gifted friends. Thanks also to my research assistants Kathleen Peggar and Amy Connor and to many friends who gave me their favorite quotations. I'm much obliged to the research librarians at Harvard's Widener Library, especially Barbara Burg. I'd like to thank my wonderful agent Jane Dystel. Thank you to my editors at Hyperion, Laurie Abkemeier and Mary Ellen O'Neill, for their enthusiasm and thoughtful suggestions. My deepest appreciation to Andrew Szanton for his numerous contributions and insightful editing. A special thanks to Michael and Justine who bring me so much joy. Most of all, thank you to my mother, Mary Chernov, for her talented artwork and loving support.

Contents

Introduction XV

PART ONE: MAPS FOR THE MIND

1.	Chart a Course for Enlightenment	3
2.	Believe	5
3.	Be Open to Grace	7
4.	Nourish Joy	9
5.	Practice Gratitude	11
6.	Cultivate Devotion	13
7.	Have Faith	15
8.	Live in Awe	17
9.	Use Affirmations	19
10.	Forgive Yourself	21
11.	Have a Crisis of Faith	23
12.	Accept What You Cannot Change	25
13.	Never Give Up Hope	27
14.	View Your Life as a Spiritual Journey	29

15. Just Be   31
16. Persist   32
17. Be Angry with God   34
18. Doubt God   36
19. Let Go   38
20. Conquer Loneliness   40
21. Grow Through Loss   42
22. Transform Your Suffering   44
23. Treat Your Life with Reverence   46
24. Savor Silence   48
25. Understand Why Your Life Is Hard   50
26. Read Good Books   52
27. Recognize the Power of Thought   54
28. Visualize   56
29. Have Compassion for Yourself   58
30. Live in the Present Moment   60

PART TWO: MAPS FOR THE BODY

31. Align Yourself with Abundance   65
32. Savor the Inner Light   67

33. Savor the Outer Light   69
34. Create a Sacred Place   71
35. Give   73
36. Make Your Body a Temple   75
37. Follow Your Heart   77
38. Experience the Rapture of Being Alive   79
39. Love Yourself   81
40. Do the Thing You Fear   83
41. Watch for Miracles   85
42. Realize the Power of Habits   87
43. Find Peace   89
44. Take Refuge in Spiritual Teachings   91
45. Keep Good Company   93
46. Find God in Nature   95
47. Renew Yourself with Exercise   97
48. Make a Pilgrimage   99
49. Simplify   101
50. Discover the Purpose of Your Journey   103
51. Get Your Prayers Answered   105
52. Transcend Toxic People   107
53. Find Your True Vocation   109

54. Go on a Retreat — 111
55. Spread Kindness — 113
56. Lighten Up — 115
57. Seek Peak Experiences — 117
58. Make Your Home a Refuge — 119
59. Design Your Own Map — 121
60. Walk to Meditate — 123
61. Practice Yoga — 126
62. Learn the Secret to Success — 128
63. Create and Savor Rituals — 130
64. Find Your Center — 132
65. Create Prosperity — 134

PART THREE: MAPS FOR THE SOUL

66. Follow Your Bliss — 139
67. Invite an Angel into Your Life — 141
68. Ask God for Help — 143
69. Watch for Signs and Wonders — 145
70. Give Your Life the Highest Vision — 147
71. Make a Connection — 149

72. Savor Spiritual Friendships   151
73. Nourish Your Relationships   153
74. Call God to You   155
75. Know That Love Waits for You   157
76. Know That You Are Never Alone   159
77. Find Community   161
78. Find Heaven Within   163
79. Nourish Your Soul with Music   165
80. Give Thanks to a Higher Power   167
81. Talk with God   169
82. Listen Deeply   171
83. Write a Letter to God   173
84. Sing to God   175
85. Crave God   177
86. Learn Love Meditation   179
87. Watch for Saints   181
88. Give Service   183
89. Love   185
90. Reimagine God   187
91. Meditate   189
92. Have Compassion for Others   191

93.	Know That Love Survives Death	193
94.	Heal Your Heartaches	195
95.	Forgive Others	197
96.	Surrender Your Problem to a Higher Power	199
97.	Prepare for Eternity	201
98.	Recognize Teachers	203
99.	Know That God Works Through Others	205
100.	Trust	207

Suggested Reading   209

Sources   212

Credits   217

INTRODUCTION

This book began the day I found a map that changed my life.

The map I found was a spiritual quotation by Joseph Campbell: "I say follow your bliss and don't be afraid, and doors will open where you didn't know they were going to be." I wrote this quote down on a piece of paper and placed it on my refrigerator where I could see it every day. I decided to live each day by that quote and to see what happened. And something did happen. With all my heart, I started to pursue what I love most—spirituality and writing. It led me to work I loved and to greater happiness and prosperity than I'd ever known. I've learned that to find real joy and transformation, we must not only find the right map but have the grace to apply its wisdom to everyday life.

All over the world, in every country, in every language, in every religion, seekers are finding the Spirit and sharing it. In *Pathways to the*

Spirit, I have collected some of their secrets. These secrets contain profound lessons for nourishing your soul and creating joy in daily life. Each quotation is followed by easy, practical tips and specific activities to put the thought into daily practice. In fact, there are hundreds of proven suggestions for connecting to the Spirit and cultivating inner joy and outer abundance.

In my travels to hundreds of churches, meditation centers, and spiritual groups around the country, I have been struck by people's widespread dismay with organized religion. Like me, many long for a spiritual group that keeps pace with the changes in society, that understands their suffering, and is relevant to their daily lives. Much as William James predicted a century ago, people are creating personal religions from a mosaic of sources and teachers. This, in many ways, is a wondrous and liberating thing. When you create your own mosaic, you can cast off religious dogma or patriarchal structures. You can choose a spiritual path that affirms your authentic self.

But "flying solo" has its risks. Hundreds have left the religions of their childhood only to find themselves feeling adrift, longing for the sense of community and connection that religion brings. They remember with a pang of loss the awesome organ music of their childhood, the sight of a packed church on Christmas Eve, the security of a spiritual foundation.

So what is to be done? Those of us piecing together a personal religion must share our ideas for practice with one another to stay connected to a community and keep our spiritual practices alive. It's crucial that we, too, feel rooted to spiritual traditions. This book is meant to be a comfort and encouragement for anyone who has ever felt alienated by organized religion but still craves spirituality in his or her life. *Pathways to the Spirit* is for anyone who wants specific activities to nourish spiritual practice. I offer it to you in the spirit of Thich Nhat Hanh's words, "We can be nourished by the best values and practices from many traditions."

Just as you have a choice of many routes on a road map, *Pathways to the Spirit* gives you a rich array of choices to nurture spiritual life. I have selected the quotations and tips listed here from a broad range of sources—eastern and western, ancient and modern. Pick and choose your favorite practices.

Gathering the best jewels from different religions can be a wondrous experience and a thrilling adventure. May this book help you discover practices that you'll return to daily for spiritual nourishment. May you find a map that guides you to your own experiences of bliss. In the words of Marie de Floris, "May hunting God be a great adventure."

PART ONE

MAPS

FOR THE

MIND

1

CHART A COURSE FOR ENLIGHTENMENT

[Enlightenment] . . . is a state of mind or consciousness, not a place some-

where, like heaven. It is right here, in the midst of the turmoil of life . . .

a center of quietness within.

—JOSEPH CAMPBELL

*   Enlightenment, or nirvana, is reserved not only for a few.
It is available to anyone in the present moment.

* Set your course for your own enlightened center. Search for the wisdom, books, and spiritual teachers that will help you reach it.

* Over morning coffee or tea, choose a spiritual principle to weave into your day. Select a teaching that brings you love and puts you in touch with a sense of mystery.

* Improve yourself each day—learn something new, meditate one minute longer, love yourself more. Resolve to raise your consciousness and to touch the Sacred each day.

2

BELIEVE

Change your thoughts and you change your world.

—NORMAN VINCENT PEALE

* If we knew the true power of belief and positive thinking, we would never have a negative thought.

* All manifestation begins with thought. The thoughts and images in our subconscious mind create our lives.

* Create an exalted vision for your life. Sit in meditation for a few minutes. Close your eyes and bring a desired goal into your mind. Affirm your desire to attract that goal to you. Say to your subconscious mind, "I am now attracting my ideal

partner." Or "I am now attracting work I love." The power of your mind will create an opportunity for you to manifest your vision.

* To reach your goal, couple unswerving belief with commitment to a series of action steps. Never doubt that with action, belief, and persistence you will achieve your goal.

3

BE OPEN TO GRACE

Grace is nothing else but a certain beginning of [God] in us.

—ST. THOMAS AQUINAS

* We're always in God's love and grace. Rarely do we realize it. Jesus said, "The kingdom of heaven is upon earth but men's eyes do not see it."

* Miracles are God's calling cards, engraved invitations to belief.

* Grace, the unmerited favor and love from God, enters our lives when we don't know how we'll get by.

* Ask God for His grace: pour your heart out to Him; ask and believe; bear your disappointments and how much you need a "grace break."

* Expand your gratitude for everything in the world and you will discover more grace. Gratitude keeps grace flowing through your life.

* Don't give up before your miracles happen. Keep speaking to God from the bottom of your heart, and grace will come.

4

NOURISH JOY

Joy is the most infallible sign of the presence of God.

—LÉON BLOY

* Joy is the soul made visible.

* Pay attention to the activities and people you most enjoy. What are you doing? Whom are you with? When you feel joy, you are closer to the Divine Presence.

* Let go of limiting beliefs. Spirit wants you to have joy, love, and prosperity beyond your wildest dreams.

* Picture yourself looking back on your life from your deathbed.

When you look back, what do you wish you did more of?
Now do it.

* Learn to nurture seeds of joy within yourself. Ask yourself,
"What's one action that I can take to increase joy today?"

PRACTICE GRATITUDE

The game was to just find something about everything to be glad about—

no matter what 'twas . . . You see, when you're hunting for the glad things,

you sort of forget the other kind.

—POLLYANNA, *POLLYANNA*

* Gratitude connects us to the joy and riches that are already in our lives.

* Make gratitude a habit. Whenever you find yourself in a bad situation, find at least one positive aspect to the situation.

* Start a gratitude journal. Write down five things you are grateful for each day.

* Each day make a mental note of something that's "not wrong." You don't have a toothache today. Your eyesight is good today. Whatever it may be.

* When you cultivate gratitude, you become a happier, more fulfilled person. The more you're grateful for, the more blessings will come to you.

CULTIVATE DEVOTION

That Supreme . . . in whom all beings abide and by whom the entire

universe is pervaded, can be attained . . . by whole-souled devotion.

—BHAGAVAD GITA 8:22

* God notices love wherever it alights.

* In Hindu scriptures, love and devotion are so powerful that
they can change your karma. If you don't like your karma,
create new karma by filling your life with love and devotion
and watch the good things that begin to unfold.

* When you've lost touch with Spirit, feel bankrupt inside and in need of connection, use devotion to find your way back. Devotion restores our connection to God and to the present moment. Where there is devotion or love, there is God.

* Another aspect of devotion is surrender. We may surrender to God's will with the prayer, "O Divine Sculptor, chisel thou my life according to thy design." When you are enduring a test, let go. Trust that God is there with you. He is always there. Know that you are never alone and that God has a divine plan for you.

HAVE FAITH

I prefer to think of faith, as Coleridge says of poetry,

not as the taking up of belief but as "the willing suspension of

disbelief" . . . a willingness to be open, to explore, to investigate.

—SHARON SALZBERG

* When we plant a seed, we don't keep digging up the soil to see if it's growing.

* Faith sometimes requires great courage. Take a risk and trust.

* Be open to a power greater than yourself.

* When you feel confused and don't know what to do, relax and trust that you will be taken care of.

LIVE IN AWE

Awe enables us to perceive in the world intimations of the divine,

to sense in small things the beginning of infinite significance,

to sense the ultimate in the common and the simple;

to feel in the rush of the passing the stillness of the eternal.

—ABRAHAM JOSHUA HESCHEL

*   Open yourself to reverence, wonder, and awe.

*   When we glimpse the Divine, awe is the natural response, for the Divine is more profound and mysterious than anything we could ever comprehend.

* Watch for glimpses of the divine order. Find those experiences, sights, and sounds which fill you with awe. Any experience met with awe can be spiritual: a safari through an animal kingdom, taking in a sunset, a hike to an awesome mountaintop.

* Reflect on the vastness of God's creation. Look for wonder and beauty in nature. Appreciate the beauty and mystery of the human mind and soul, of the Mona Lisa, of a shooting star on a summer evening. Think of the inventions the human mind has created.

* Look for glimpses of the Divine in daily life and ways that the radiant pours itself into this world.

USE AFFIRMATIONS

"I am" is the strongest creative statement in the universe . . . "I am" sets

into motion those experiences, calls them forth, brings them to you.

—NEALE DONALD WALSCH

* Charge your affirmation with power; see yourself living your goal in the present.

* Trust that the universe is bringing your most cherished desire to you, and that when the timing is right, your dream will manifest.

* Affirmation and unswerving belief are two of the most power-

ful creative forces in the universe for achieving your heart's desires and creating a life you love.

* Change your thoughts and you can change your whole life. Our thoughts form a powerful blueprint in our subconscious minds.

FORGIVE YOURSELF

How unhappy is he who cannot forgive himself.

—PUBLILIUS SYRUS

* Never let anyone trap you in a sterile perfectionism. Realize that you can't always say the right words to someone or handle every situation with grace.

* Forgive yourself for not having your life exactly as you want it.

* Accept failure. Learn from it. Experiment around it.

* Know that compassion for others begins with being able to accept and forgive yourself. As long as you judge others for

their imperfections, you will never be able to truly accept and love yourself.

* Accept all of your feelings. If you have intense feelings of anger or hatred toward someone, which you are ashamed about, realize that they are only feelings and that there must be a good reason for them. Next, drop any judgments you have about these feelings. If you can accept them, you can begin to transform them.

* See if you can soften your heart and feel compassion for yourself. We grow when we focus on the good in ourselves and others.

11

HAVE A CRISIS
OF FAITH

My God, my God, why hast thou forsaken me?

—MATTHEW 27:46, KING JAMES VERSION (KJV)

* Try to relax when you have a crisis of faith. Everyone, including Jesus and the saints, has occasionally lost faith. Alternating phases of faith and doubt are a natural part of spiritual life.

* When you're going through a crisis of faith, place your life in God's hands. Trust that the highest good for your life is unfolding.

* If your faith was once deep, that same seed of faith is within you. When the faithless period passes, your lost seeds of faith will flourish again.

* Reframe: A crisis of faith isn't sent to cripple you, but is a chance to grow. "Hitting bottom" can spur you on to new growth and to enact more sustaining solutions to recurring problems.

* Valuable lessons often come to us only after a crisis of faith. A soul-wrenching crisis can lead to deeper personal growth in relationships, finances, and the Spirit. We may discover exciting new spiritual paths that better suit us, a healthier relationship, or a better job.

1 2

ACCEPT WHAT YOU CANNOT CHANGE

Our entire life . . . consists ultimately of accepting ourselves as we are.

—JEAN ANOUILH

* Resistance to suffering, not suffering itself, is what brings the greatest pain.

* It takes courage to uncover your pain and to touch all of your feelings with compassion. But it's one of the most important habits you'll ever learn.

* Become aware of your resistance to daily reality. When you find

yourself resisting, gently note this fact. Soften your heart. Buddhist teacher Jack Kornfield advises us to ask ourselves, "What wants acceptance?"

* Fighting life only saps our energy, blocking us from the love, healing, and compassion available to us from our own hearts. Once we accept our given reality, our energy shifts. Release happens.

* Can you accept your life exactly as it is? Embrace your worst fear—and fear will recede.

1 3

NEVER GIVE UP HOPE

Sometimes I go about in pity for myself, and all the while

A great wind is bearing me across the sky.

—OJIBWA SAYING

* No one is doomed to failure but the pessimist.

* Try these three keys to restoring hope:

  — Stay in the present moment.
  — Find a project to absorb your mind and give you a sense of purpose.
  — Focus only on the hour in front of you. *Take one day at a time,* and then go to bed early.

* When life feels unbearable, when you don't know how the bills will get paid, when you've lost the love of your life, when your career feels at a dead end, recruit a support team. Be uplifted by their strength and faith in you.

* Life is profoundly cyclical. The wheel never stops turning. No matter how dark the night, morning comes. No matter how cold the winter, spring comes. Why despair over only part of the cycle?

* Create your own momentum. Keep pursuing your dreams until they come true. Jesus said, "Those who seek should not stop seeking until they find." (Thomas 2:1, Scholar's Version (SV))

* Never give up. Some dreams are a long time in coming.

1 4

VIEW YOUR LIFE AS A
SPIRITUAL JOURNEY

It is good to have an end to journey toward; but it is the

journey that matters in the end.

—URSULA KROEBER LE GUIN

* The spiritual journey is an adventure to find ways to make daily life richer.

* What kinds of feelings and experiences do you want on your journey? Enchantment, mystical experiences, meaning? An

assurance of safety? Love from God? William James wanted "the feeling that great and wondrous things are in the air."

* Pack a treasure map for your journey. This is a collection of spiritual treasures and jewels that can guide you on such a journey. Keep favorite spiritual books by your bedside; write down inspiring spiritual quotations; spend time with favorite religious groups or teachers.

* Reflect on your journey. Write a journal entry about your spiritual life. What are its turning points? What groups have you belonged to? Who are your favorite teachers and why? If you left certain groups, why did you leave? How does your own brand of spirituality shape your everyday life? What is your vision of spirituality? If you could design the perfect spiritual path or group for yourself, what would you create?

* And, finally, when you have done all these things, share this exercise with a friend. Exchanging stories about your spiritual journeys creates connection and gives you inspiration.

* Above all, find or create a spiritual path that honors your most authentic self.

15

JUST BE

If all beings are Buddha, why all this striving?

—DOGEN ZENJI

* Whenever you're feeling fearful or sad, take refuge in the practice of mindfulness. As you breathe in and out, let go of pain about the past and fear of the future.

* Give yourself a weekly "Just Be" vacation. Designate Fridays as a day where you don't try to improve anything about your life. Fully accept yourself just as you are. Love and be nice to yourself. Savor the peace, joy, and love that come through just being.

* Serenity means not having to change anything about the present moment.

1 6

PERSIST

No matter how impossible of accomplishment his goal may seem,

the man of [intention] never stops repeating conscious acts of

determination to achieve it, as long as he lives.

—PARAMAHANSA YOGANANDA

* Persistence and willpower open up unlimited possibilities for success. When you set an intention in your mind and persist, you send out certain vibrations to which the universe then responds by creating favorable conditions.

* Don't give up hope after one or two failed efforts. To realize your intention, take a series of determined actions until you

manifest your heart's desire. Mark Victor Hansen, author of *Chicken Soup for the Soul*, was previously a geodesic dome salesman, who had to declare bankruptcy before discovering and persisting in his new career as a motivational speaker and author. His books have sold more than 30 million copies.

* Develop persistence. First, set and accomplish small goals. Later, build on your success by setting and reaching larger goals.

* Don't let fear of success stop you from achieving your goals. Know that you possess the ability to handle the changes that come with success.

BE ANGRY WITH GOD

The God I believe in is not so fragile that you hurt Him

by being angry at Him, or so petty that He will hold it

against you for being upset with Him.

— RABBI HAROLD KUSHNER

* Anger is a healthy part of love relationships.

* It's okay to feel angry at God.

* A loving God is a good listener and takes the time to hear all of your feelings.

* God wants you to recognize and express all of your feelings. A true friend, like God, won't run away because you express dissatisfaction or anger.

* Millions of people have been angry at God and felt abandoned. When they told God they couldn't stand the pain anymore and had to give up—sometimes the instant after they had given up hope—then God's miracle came.

* Accept your anger and let it flow. Tell God you've had to give up; then watch for God's miracle.

1 8

DOUBT GOD

How long, O Lord? Wilt thou forget me forever?

How long wilt thou hide thy face from me? How long must I bear

pain in my soul, and have sorrow in my heart all the day?

—PSALM 13:1–2, REVISED STANDARD VERSION (RSV)

* Have a crisis of faith and don't be afraid to feel that God has forsaken you. It worked for Jesus.

* The deep fear and desperation of Jesus got God's attention. It can get a lot of attention for you, too.

*   Make a list of the times you felt desperate; and then you prayed, and received the help and support you needed. Know that God never gives you more than you can handle.

*   Use the hero myth. The hero leaves home to search for answers on how to live, encounters adversity, despairs, and finds his way back. On the return journey, the hero comes back stronger, more noble, and wise. Every one of us has come back from a dark night of the soul. Each of us is a hero of his/her own life story.

1 9

LET GO

Focus on what you are moving toward rather

than what you are leaving behind.

—ALAN COHEN

* Are you holding on to something in your past? Why not totally let go?

* Letting go is difficult. We resist change and want to hold on to the past. We are afraid of the unknown. Yet impermanence is a truth of life. Change is a natural rhythm.

* When you let go, you make room for something better to come along. Just as God's power and God's love are stronger than any-

thing humans can imagine, so are his plans often more profound than we can imagine.

* Stop fighting life and learn to go with the flow. Master the art of letting go and you'll be happier, more peaceful. Achaan Chah says, "Let go a little to have a little peace. Let go a lot to have a lot of peace."

* The saying "Let go and let God" is a way to calm ourselves after we've done everything we can about a particular problem. It doesn't mean that we simply sit back and do nothing. It means that we make our best effort and then leave matters in the hands of a Higher Power.

* Happiness comes through enjoying and being absorbed in the process rather than focusing on the goal and what you can get out of it.

20

CONQUER LONELINESS

The knowledge that close friends and relatives are there for us . . . is more

important than the actual number of social contacts that we have.

—RICHARD SCHWARTZ AND JACQUELINE OLDS

* Loneliness plagues many people today, regardless of age, economic circumstances, or marital status. In a recent survey in *Psychology Today*, more than half of the subjects reported feeling lonely.

* Remember that loneliness is a feeling and it, too, shall pass.

* It takes planning and ingenuity to keep loneliness at bay, but it's one of the best uses of your energy and time. For when you

decrease loneliness, you increase joy, love, and connection and reduce depression. People with support systems and active social networks live longer, healthier lives.

* Take actions to overcome your loneliness. Try reading two good books on loneliness, such as *Overcoming Loneliness* by Richard Schwartz and *Intimate Connections* by David Burns. Try support groups, book groups, or volunteer work.

* Remember that you have a Divine Partner.

* Give yourself the nurturing, compassion, and support that you want a partner to give you.

* Do the "twenty-minute connection"—set a timer each day for a "make connections" time. During this time, telephone old friends, reach out to new acquaintances, make fun weekend plans.

21

GROW THROUGH LOSS

Every exit is an entry somewhere else.

—TOM STOPPARD

* In painful situations filled with loss, first send compassion to yourself.

* People think that something's wrong with them when they aren't feeling happy. They feel they must escape from suffering. However, the first and second noble truths of Buddhism tell us that life is suffering and everything is impermanent and changing. No one can escape from suffering. Recognize loss as impermanence.

* Think of your life journey as a series of lessons. Ask "What am I supposed to learn here?"

* Never expect improvement to be constant. If improvement is constant, the task is too easy. If you can take two steps forward for every one step back, you're doing well.

* Loss helps us to feel compassion for others.

* Feel fully the depth of your sorrow. The only way out of pain is through it.

22

TRANSFORM YOUR SUFFERING

The chief pang of most trials is not so much the actual suffering

itself as our own spirit of resistance to it.

—JEAN NICOLAS GROU

There is no such thing as a problem without a gift for you in its hands.

You seek problems because you need their gifts.

—RICHARD BACH

* First, identify the feeling. Are you feeling angry, sad, hurt, or afraid?

* Try mindful breathing while you sit with the feelings. Feel them and let them go. Again and again, in rhythm. Picture them physically leaving your body as you feel them.

* Care for your feelings with the same tenderness that you would lavish on a child's feelings. Be present with the feeling. Offer yourself comforting, soothing words: "You will be all right." "It's okay."

* You cannot transform feelings until you fully accept and face them. Use your curiosity about them to help you explore them. As you accept them, their energy dissipates. They turn into something else. The feelings pass.

* View your problems as your teachers. What lesson does the problem have for you? Affirm that this is the life you intended to live. Can you say "yes" to your whole life, including the suffering?

TREAT YOUR LIFE
WITH REVERENCE

For every thing that lives is Holy, life delights in life.

— WILLIAM BLAKE

* The very ground you stand upon is sacred. Sacred ground is wherever you dwell with awareness. Sacred ground is wherever you choose it to be.

* Pretend you are a Zen master. The next time you enter a room, enter slowly, mindfully, with a kind of deep attention that borders on reverence. This attitude can sanctify the room and the moment.

* Every day select one activity and ask yourself, "How can I do this more mindfully?"

* Reverence deepens our appreciation for life. Reverence infuses the ordinary with something sacred.

* Cultivate a reverence for the minute particulars of your life—a clean home, clean air to breathe, clean water to drink, and kind neighbors.

* Look for radiance in nature, in your loved ones, in your home. Smell a rose, look into the eyes of a child, fill your home with art, or watch a sunset.

2 4

SAVOR SILENCE

Be still, and know that I am God.

—PSALM 46:10, KJV

* Silence is a wonderful thing. It is organic, and it can be rich and prolific.

* Does silence bring you anxiety? If so, reflect on why this should be so.

* Some people prefer a monkish silence, being cloistered. Others prefer to worship or meditate in silent groups.

* Set aside an hour every day to be still and become peaceful. Silence is a time to rejuvenate, reflect, and renew.

* The best time to commune with God is through the silence of meditation. Many people talk to God, but how many people listen? Carry the inner stillness of meditation with you throughout the day.

* In April, join "turn off the TV week." Unplug the phone. Eat a meal in silent meditation.

* If you feel stressed, take a few minutes for a short walk outside. If age or poor weather make walking difficult, take an "interior journey" and write in your journal.

UNDERSTAND WHY
YOUR LIFE IS HARD

Unless we agree to suffer we cannot be free from suffering.

—D.T. SUZUKI

* Life is hard. Most of the world's great sages have said so. The Buddha taught the Four Noble Truths. The first one was: "Life is suffering."

* M. Scott Peck in his classic *The Road Less Traveled* begins this way: "Life is difficult. This is a great truth . . ." But Peck goes on to say that once we accept that life is difficult, this fact will no longer trouble us.

* As hard as it may be to accept, life has been, is today, and always will be, hard for every human being who honestly faces life.

* Realize that your suffering has meaning and purpose. It has made you more compassionate to others' suffering. You can now use your pain to help others overcome suffering.

* Those people you know who seem happier than you—they may not be. People take care to hide their pain and doubt, even from friends.

* Get plenty of support. Talk out your problems with others. Find a support group. Doctors find that cancer patients who join support groups live longer. Listen to others' stories of suffering. Remember the adage, "A pain shared is a pain halved."

2 6

READ GOOD BOOKS

All that mankind has done, thought, gained or been: it is lying

as in magic preservation in the pages of books.

—THOMAS CARLYLE

* Books are dense with the past. Books conjure up whole new worlds. They insulate us against self-pity and despair by telling us so much that we yearn to know.

* Good books are a great aid on the spiritual path. They offer a world of solace, expert advice, and guidance for your life journey.

* Read inspirational literature each day. Try reading scriptures, the lives of the saints, or any book that teaches you something new.

* Reading makes people feel good. On happiness surveys, people rate reading as one of the activities that makes them feel happiest.

* When you're feeling down, bury yourself in a good book. As one saint said, "Books are our silent perpetual friends."

27

RECOGNIZE THE
POWER OF THOUGHT

We magnetize into our lives whatever we hold in our thought.

—RICHARD BACH

* Realize the incredible power of your mind to shape your life.

* After near-death experiences, people report learning that thought is the single most powerful creative force in their lives. God and our subconscious mind build our lives according to our thoughts and beliefs.

* Track your thoughts. Every thought sows a seed for Spirit to

bring to fruition. Whatever you believe and focus on, you will manifest.

* In prayer or meditation, affirm, "God and I are one." Tell God what you seek to build in your life.

* You have within you all of the strength and wisdom you could ever need. Never doubt that. Never fear to draw upon it.

* Judgments about ourselves or negative thoughts about our future can cause depression. Beware of thoughts that revolve around the words "never" or "always."

2 8

VISUALIZE

Visualization means to create a mental picture of ourselves as we would like to be, to hand this picture over to the universal Law for execution and to believe implicitly that it will act.

—ERNEST HOLMES

* Visualization is one of the most powerful creative forces in the universe. To visualize, you can use either words or images.

* First, select a goal that you want to achieve. Then find or compose a quotation that captures the essence of what you want to create. Place the quotation where you can look at it every day.

This allows it to seep into your subconscious mind, where it can begin to shape your everyday life.

* Then once a week, close your eyes and make a mental picture of your goal. See yourself living this dream in the present.

* Release your desire to the universe. *Believe* it will happen.

* Take a series of discreet actions to achieve your goal.

* Model your actions after someone who has achieved a similar goal.

* Surround yourself with people who believe in your dream and want to help you achieve it.

* Another great way to tap into the power of visualization is to make a treasure map. Buy a blank journal or sketch pad and make a collage of your ideal life. Cut out pictures and phrases from magazines to create a personal treasure map. Watch your life, almost miraculously, begin to align with the images on your treasure map.

* Use a journal to write down your ideal life. Record entries as though you are actually living them. If you want to meet your soul mate, write down the kinds of topics you might discuss with this person. Write about how you would spend an ideal workday.

29

HAVE COMPASSION
FOR YOURSELF

As we learn to have compassion for ourselves, the circle of

compassion for others becomes wider.

—PEMA CHÖDRÖN

* Your compassion must include yourself to be complete.

* As soon as someone harms you, immediately send compassion
  to yourself. Acknowledge the hurt you feel. During meditation
  or quiet time, give yourself loving kindness phrases like, "May I

be well. May I be happy." Try to send yourself love from your own heart.

* Practice accepting all of your feelings. The next time you feel lonely or hurt, embrace your pain rather than judging it or backing away.

30

LIVE IN THE
PRESENT MOMENT

You will find rest from vain fancies if you do every act in life

as though it were your last.

—MARCUS AURELIUS

* Live too much in the past or in the future, and you lose touch
  with the present moment. This moment will never come again.
  Live in the now.

* Buddhists use the breath to come back to the present.
  Whenever you feel sad or frightened, use your breathing to
  return to the present moment. Align your breath with a phrase

such as "Peace." Fear is, in most cases, a symptom of either dwelling in the past or future.

* Make an appointment with the present moment. Throughout your day, stop and take a few minutes to observe your surroundings. Breathe, relax, and appreciate the life that's right in front of you.

* Cultivate awareness of things in your daily life—your breath, the sky, the sight of tree branches with new spring leaves. Recite the name of the objects in front of you to make them more real. As you pick up your coffee cup or open your laptop, say the words drinking "coffee," or "opening laptop."

* Express yourself in the moment. Don't hold on to your feelings. Express them to people as they arise. Then you'll live in the now.

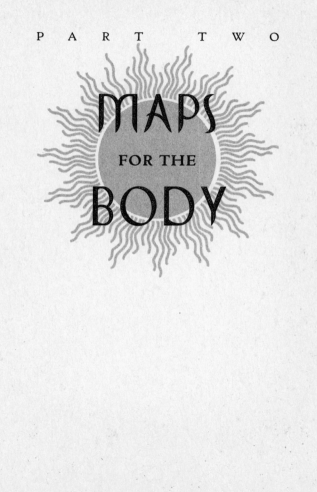

PART TWO

MAPS
FOR THE
BODY

31

ALIGN YOURSELF
WITH ABUNDANCE

Abundance is, in large part, an attitude.

—SUE PATTON THOELE

* Make relationships and love your number one priority, and you will be rich.

* To create more abundance, first rid your mind of all thoughts of failure. Affirm that you are now open and ready to receive the good that is now yours.

*   Keep a gratitude journal. The more you give thanks and praise for what's already in your life, the more you create a channel for further abundance to come to you. Gratitude journals connect us to the joy and plenty that already enrich our lives.

SAVOR THE

INNER LIGHT

With all your science can you tell me how it is,

and whence it is, that the light comes into the soul?

—HENRY DAVID THOREAU

* The Religious Society of Friends (the Quakers) speaks of cultivating "the inner light"—the spark of divinity that each of us has.

* Quakers encourage us to approach God directly, without need of ministers, priests, or gurus.

* Following the inner light is not only simple and practical but can be mystical.

* Begin an inner light journal. This is a blank book that you fill with activities and ideas for cultivating your inner light. Playing tennis. Mountain climbing. Drawing. Reading scriptures. Nurturing your inner light is one of the most important things you can learn on your life's journey.

* Begin an inner light journal for a child, and help a child discover her inner light. Record the activities that your child gravitates toward. Patterns of the child's favorite skills will emerge in the journal. Share the journal with your child as she grows older and begins searching for a vocation.

33

SAVOR THE

OUTER LIGHT

Truly the light is sweet, and a pleasant thing it is

for the eyes to behold the sun.

—ECCLESIASTES 11:7, KJV

* Do you feel more downcast during the winter months? We often attribute the "winter blues" to winter flu or cold, or to wet weather. But often we are missing light itself.

* Try to rise earlier in the winter to get an extra hour or so of morning light. Go to bed earlier, if need be. In late winter,

remind yourself that each day brings a little more light than the day before.

* The Incas, South American Indians who ruled an enormous empire in the early sixteenth century, had a state religion that centered around the sun.

* The Aztec Indians of fifteenth-century Mexico believed that the sun was the giver of life, including the body.

* Studies have shown that sunlight effectively reduces levels of depression. Take a five-to-ten minute sunbath each day to increase your energy. Keep your sunbaths brief to avoid undue exposure to the sun's destructive rays. But do take in the healing rays of the sun to wipe away fatigue and uplift your mood.

34

CREATE A
SACRED PLACE

You must have a room or a certain hour of the day where you

do not know what was in the morning paper . . . a place where you

can simply experience and bring forth what you are, and what you might

be . . . At first you may find nothing's happening . . . But if you have a

sacred place and use it, take advantage of it, something will happen.

—JOSEPH CAMPBELL

* To create a sacred space, select an area of your home and fill it with objects that are meaningful to you—a comfortable mohair blanket, family photographs, your favorite inspirational books, a soothing CD. Have at least one object there to remind you of the mystical.

* If you have a writing desk, studio, or other creative space, hang a photograph of a saint, writer, or teacher who inspires you.

* Devote a half hour a day in your sacred space to what you think is your sacred work. Over time you will be amazed at the transformation your life undergoes.

* Sacred space can also be a time of day. Reserve at least one hour each day to do something that nourishes you. Play your favorite game, read for fun, socialize with a friend, or enjoy a hobby.

35

GIVE

The fragrance always remains in the hand that gives the rose.

—HEDA BEJAR

* Those who give most, receive most. Reaching out and giving to others is how we keep abundance circulating in our lives.

* Expressing kindness or generosity toward someone blesses you with another human connection.

* Give a gift to someone—a smile, a thoughtful card, or interest expressed in someone's life. In one laugh shared with a stranger, you never know how much you might be cheering someone up.

*   Giving fills us as much as it fills the other person.

*   Realize that generosity is an important ingredient for your own happiness.

3 6

MAKE YOUR

BODY A TEMPLE

If anything is sacred, the human body is sacred.

— WALT WHITMAN

* Accept your body. Your body is a temple for the Holy Spirit, a carrier of divine spark. Learn to trust the wisdom of your body.

* Treat your body as a "thou." Get in touch with your inner divinity. Treat others' bodies as a thou to honor their inner divinity.

* When you damage your body, you damage your consciousness. Follow the Buddhist precept of ingesting only items that preserve peace and joy in your body and in your consciousness. Ingesting toxins such as alcohol, drugs, and violent TV programs severs the connection between you and your inner light.

* Find delight on the path to Spirit. Cultivate joy in your body: exercise, make love, get a massage, or practice yoga.

* The real purpose of your body is to fulfill a divine plan that was chosen by you and by God before you were born. Discover what your purpose is here on earth.

* Thank your body for all the service it has given you. Say:
"Thank you to my eyes for all the beautiful things I see."
"Thank you to my body that I may enjoy physical movement."
"Thank you to my mind that I may read and reflect."
"Thank you for the love and joy I have been able to give to others."

FOLLOW YOUR HEART

Pointing directly at your own heart, you find Buddha.

—BODHIDHARMA

* Every major religion tells us that God can be found through the heart.

* The heart is a vehicle that can transform suffering into joy.

* Realize that the love you've been searching for is within you. Once you open to the love in your heart, you will see love and goodness everywhere.

* Remember that God's love is large enough to contain all life's pain, hurts, and disappointments.

* Open your heart no matter how many times fear has closed it. Choose love, not fear.

* Remember that whenever you need guidance, you can draw on a presence within. Look to your own heart for love and for the answers. When you learn to trust yourself and your own intuition, you will find peace.

EXPERIENCE THE RAPTURE
OF BEING ALIVE

So many people don't know how to inspire themselves.

Use everything that moves you: music, walking by water, flowers,

photographs of the enlightened ones. Inspiration helps so deeply in

overcoming laziness, and summons what the Sufis call the fragrance

of the Beloved into everything.

—ANDREW HARVEY

* In Hindu scriptures, one of the words used for God is "bliss." Bliss or rapture is believed to be a direct experience of God, if not an actual experience of God.

* Follow your intuition of where your rapture is. Keep a journal of what you're doing when you feel happiest. Do these things as often as possible.

* Messages about what you love most may come through in subtle ways. Listen to your inclinations and inner voice. Fulfill unfinished dreams. Something inside you knows what you love. Determine what this is and don't be afraid to follow it.

* Discover your rapture and you will resonate in your innermost being. Again and again, you will see that your life has a purpose, that you are living the life you were meant to live. Your rapture is what gives you a flow experience, a feeling of being so absorbed in an activity that you lose all sense of time and feel only exhilaration.

* Make a list of activities to enhance your sense of aliveness. Include physical experiences such as games or sports, actions to deepen sensual experience, and ways to express your emotions.

39

LOVE YOURSELF

According to the Buddha, you can search throughout the entire universe for someone who is more deserving of your love and affection than you are yourself, and that person is not to be found anywhere. You yourself, as much as anybody in the entire universe, deserve your love and affection.

—SHARON SALZBERG

* How can we love someone else if we can't feel love for ourselves? The more you love yourself, the more you'll be able to love others and spread good on this planet.

* Love yourself and others will love you, too.

* God loves every single one of us, unconditionally.

* Vow to be your own best friend through difficult times.

* We cannot nourish peace in those we love until we nourish peace in ourselves.

40

DO THE THING
YOU FEAR

Stop to look fear in the face. . . . You must do the thing you cannot do.

—ELEANOR ROOSEVELT

* To remove fear or worry, analyze your fear. What specifically do you fear and why? What's the worst thing that could happen? Naming your worst fear is the first step in relinquishing its power over you. You must be willing to contact your fear, to go fully into it.

* Next, replace your fear with an image of a positive outcome.

* What precaution can you take to remove the fear and protect yourself? Or is the object of your fear extremely unlikely to happen? Ninety-five percent of our worries never come to fruition.

* Take your mind off light worries. Exercise, walk, or laugh at a comedy video.

* For heavy worries, practice deep breathing for five minutes. As your consciousness drops from the mind into the body, fear dissipates. Align your in-breath with a comforting word such as "God" or "peace." Mentally affirm that God is protecting you.

* Above all, don't worry alone. Socialize with friends. Share your worries and fears to reduce their power over you.

WATCH FOR MIRACLES

People usually consider walking on water or in thin air a miracle.

But I think the real miracle is not to walk either on water or in thin air,

but to walk on earth. Every day we are engaged in a miracle which we

don't even recognize: a blue sky, white clouds, green leaves, the black,

curious eyes of a child—our own two eyes. All is a miracle.

—THICH NHAT HANH

* Miracles are God's radiant visits to this world. Just as you cultivate an attitude of gratitude, cultivate a belief in miracles.

* Hundreds of people, in dozens of countries in every century, have left testimony of the miracles they have known. Read some of this testimony. Learn about the lives of great saints whose lives were filled with premonitions, signs, and wonders.

* Miracles are heaven-sent. They instill awe and connect us to wonder and mystery. Miracles are divine interventions sent to help us, instill hope, deeply encourage, and comfort us. They relieve our suffering and express God's compassion and love. Miracles are outward occurrences, like a healing that extends life or a turning point, but they are also a frame of mind.

* Keep a miracle journal. Buy a blank book and write down all the miracles that have filled your life and the lives of your friends. When you need a miracle, read through your journal to remind yourself that God has brought you many miracles and will continue to do so. Give thanks for the miracles that have filled your life.

* Miracles remind us how little we know of the future.

42

REALIZE THE POWER

OF HABITS

We are what we repeatedly do.

Excellence, then, is not an act, but a habit.

—ARISTOTLE

* Habits establish routine, structure, continuity, reduce tedium, and give meaning to our routines. Turning what is tedious in life into a habit gives meaning to otherwise meaningless things. Even bad habits offer the reassurance of the familiar.

* Learn to turn good habits into rituals by performing them with awareness.

* Examine your life. Identify which of your habits are beneficial and which are destructive.

* A bad habit may give temporary pleasure, but it only creates more misery in the end.

* You have the power to unlearn old patterns and develop good habits. Are you having trouble breaking a bad habit because you're a "creature of habit"? You have "an addictive personality"? All right, admit it and now substitute the bad habit with the good one.

* Find a partner to help you break bad habits. Company is stronger than willpower.

* Good habits are the ones that make us feel good about ourselves. Letting go of old patterns increases our self-confidence, sense of control, and hope for the future.

FIND PEACE

The first proof of God's presence is an ineffable peace.

—PARAMAHANSA YOGANANDA

* Peace is available in the present moment.

* Calm yourself by practicing conscious breathing. As you breathe in, say silently, "Breathing in." As you breathe out, say, "Breathing out." The Hindus call this kind of simple, sacred verbal formula, repeated over and over as a means of spiritual release, a "mantra."

* Meditate. Listen to harmonious music. Light incense or candles.

* Lie on the grass beneath a tree and look up at the sky through the branches.

* The smile of a child is one of the greatest gifts on earth. A smile is the beginning of love. Always return a child's smile with one of your own.

* Think less. Exercise for twenty minutes to slow down your thinking and rest your mind.

* Seek out company that relaxes you. Visit your favorite friend who can always comfort you and cheer you up; spend time with your favorite child.

* Be aware of what you are feeding your consciousness—violent TV dramas, news programs full of fear, toxins in your diet.

* Find time for silence. Turn off your telephone. Give up an hour of television. Curl up with a good book.

TAKE REFUGE IN
SPIRITUAL TEACHINGS

I take refuge in the Buddha

I take refuge in the Dharma

I take refuge in the Sangha

—BUDDHIST PRAYER: THE THREE JEWELS

*   In Buddhism, whenever we are agitated, stressed, afraid, or
sad, we take refuge in the Three Jewels—the Buddha (the

Enlightened One), the dharma (his teachings), and the sangha (our spiritual community).

* The Three Jewels are the riches on a spiritual treasure hunt. They offer a road map to enlightenment and a place of refuge along the way. Each religion has its own version of the Three Jewels.

* Find the jewels in your own tradition that give you strength and peace. You might take refuge in the Trinity, in Mother Mary, in Mohammed, or in the Christian practice of "resting in God." Invoke the name of your teacher, repeating his or her name again and again as a mantra. Fill your mind with the wholesome qualities of your teacher. Meditate on his or her love and compassionate actions. Then select a teaching to practice throughout your day.

* Take refuge in the teachings of your path several times a day, so the practice becomes habitual. Just knowing that the Three Jewels are there for us brings comfort and relief. When you go for refuge in the safe haven of your spiritual path, you touch the Holy Spirit.

KEEP GOOD COMPANY

Find those persons in whose presence you feel more energetic, more creative

and more able to pursue your life goals. Stay away from persons who make

you feel apprehensive, or who influence you to doubt yourself. Especially,

stay away from those persons who drain you, so that your energy is all

used up in trying to maintain the relationship.

—DENNIS F. AUGUSTINE

If we keep "wise company," as the Buddha said, and have good friends,

we have one of the greatest resources for happiness and freedom.

—SHARON SALZBERG

* Good company is a great blessing. Seek out the people in whose presence you feel uplifted and esteemed. Spend time with people who help you realize how much you can achieve.

* Choose your closest friends, business associates, and life companion with the utmost care, for they will hugely influence your happiness.

* In your gratitude journal, list all of the wonderful people in your life. Think about what is special about each of these people. The more you savor the good in your relationships, the more good company you will attract.

* The malignant moods and self-defeating thoughts of others can have a terrible impact on you. So, too, the positive thoughts and good moods of others can uplift you.

* Observe how each person treats you. Ask yourself, "Would I treat someone this way?" Beware of anyone who doesn't treat you as you treat others.

* Keeping good company causes your happiness to grow.

FIND GOD IN NATURE

Nature is full of genius, full of the divinity;

so that not a snowflake escapes its fashioning hand.

—HENRY DAVID THOREAU

The sky is the daily bread of the eyes.

—RALPH WALDO EMERSON

*   Zen Buddhism and Hinduism root God so deeply in nature
that there is no distinction between them.

* Spend some time in nature each week. Eat lunch in a beautiful place, jog around a reservoir or park, walk through a pine forest, watch the sun set over the ocean, look up at the night sky. Let yourself be enveloped by a canopy of starlight. Beauty and nature are all around us.

* Part of the reason that people fail to find God or to have deeply satisfying spiritual journeys is that they move too quickly, try to experience too much too fast, seek enlightenment overnight. When you walk in nature, take in everything around you. Walk slowly. Let the perceptions of your walk come to you. Mentally call things by their names to make them more real. Reflect on the idea that there is something much greater than the human dimension.

* While in nature, practice mindfulness. Look for beautiful things. Let nature nourish you with her abundant life and calming effects. Feel yourself wrapped in the healing and supportive arms of God.

RENEW YOURSELF

WITH EXERCISE

There are no riches above a sound body.

—ECCLESIASTICUS 30:16, RSV

* Remember that the body is the temple of the soul. Those who mistreat the body tend to mistreat the soul within. Observe vital health laws, such as exercise, healthy diet, and self-control.

* Exercise moderately three to five times a week. Regular exercise erases fatigue and energizes the body. Lack of exercise drains your vitality.

* Make time for daily exercise like walking. Exercise until you break a sweat. Daily walking is enough to keep your heart healthy.

* Exercise to elevate mood. Studies show that exercise triggers a release of endorphins, the body's natural pain reliever.

* Health researchers say that exercise produces more than thirty healthy changes in the body and mind. It has more positive physical benefits on the body than any other activity. Exercise improves the functioning of the lungs, heart, and many other vital organs and can ward off stress, depression, illness, and colds.

* Make time for relaxation. Exercise or get a massage to reduce muscle tension. We experience the radiant more easily when we are fully relaxed. Most people think of exercise as work; but actually, exercise helps us to relax.

4 8

MAKE A PILGRIMAGE

Pilgrimage . . . is the strong and steadfast aspiration to meet God

face to face.

—DILIP KUMAR ROY

* Make a pilgrimage to take a step closer to God, to tangibly connect with the divine. It can leave behind deep and permanent impressions. It can foretell great blessings to come.

* Tangible feelings of the Divine Presence pervade the places where the enlightened ones have communed with God. Tremendous vibrations of peace exist there. Visit these sacred

places to feel the Divine qualities of God—unconditional love, deep compassion, joy, and peace.

* Some of my favorite pilgrimage sites include Self-Realization Fellowship's Lake Shrine in Pacific Palisades, California; Plum Village in France, the residence of Zen master Thich Nhat Hanh; and the medieval cathedral of Chartres in France.

* A pilgrimage could transform your life. You might discover the new religious path you've been waiting for your entire life. You might meet a soul mate.

* On a pilgrimage, you set off on a journey. Feel the blessings and holy vibrations left by your spiritual teacher in this sacred place. Walk the path that your teacher walked. Pray where he or she realized God. Some go on pilgrimages to find caves in the Himalayas, some to visit famous ashrams or discover places of stunning natural beauty.

* Drink in the peace and tranquility of your sacred place. Let it fill you up. When you return home, learn to access this refuge in the midst of your hectic everyday life.

SIMPLIFY

Our life is frittered away by detail . . .

Simplify, simplify.

— HENRY DAVID THOREAU

* Simplifying is like weeding your garden. It allows you to get rid of unwanted clutter so you can appreciate the beauty of what you already have.

* Simplicity brings a sense of order, clarity of thought, and spirit of renewal. Simplicity allows us to live in a state of grace, get back to basics, find more time and energy.

* Put first things first. Prioritize. When you plan your weekly schedule, ask yourself, "What's most important?" Now set up your goals for the week based on your response to this question. Are your weekly activities aligned with the deeper purpose of your life? When you plan your day, keep "first things first" in your mind.

* Simplify your thinking. Apply a saying: "keep it simple," "one day at a time," "live in the present."

* Be aware of objects that distract you: phone calls, television, the Internet, or old memories. Set up your environment—both your surroundings and inner mental environment—to reduce distractions.

* Once we simplify, we have energy for the things that matter most.

DISCOVER THE PURPOSE
OF YOUR JOURNEY

Happiness is . . . obtained through fidelity to a worthy purpose.

—HELEN KELLER

* Before you can find happiness, you must have a purpose for living.

* Learn the art of goal planning. Goals instill purpose, order, and meaning to daily life. Goals give us something to aim for and clear steps to take. Create goals for even your mundane tasks.

Is there something that you can do faster, longer, more efficiently?

* Write a mission statement for your life. This represents the very best within you and your ideal life. A good mission statement inspires you to live the highest vision for your life. One homily I've always liked is this: "It's only a dream until you write it down. Then it's a goal." You'll be delighted and amazed at the enormous power that writing a mission statement has to change every area of your life.

* Once a year, go on a retreat. In a lovely natural setting, in a peaceful mood, and with all the insight you can muster, lovingly revise and embrace your mission statement.

* Connect to your mission statement. Read it every week and plan your daily activities with it in mind. You may notice little difference at first. But over time, dedication to this practice will profoundly transform your life.

* Why do so many people not follow their life's purpose? They may distrust their feelings about what their heart tells them they should do. Learn to trust your innermost longings. Our desires are our maps to follow the Divine's will.

GET YOUR PRAYERS
ANSWERED

What things soever ye desire when ye pray, believe ye receive them,

and ye shall have them.

— M A R K 1 1 : 2 4, K J V

* The secret of prayer is to believe that your prayer will be answered.

* Heartfelt prayers work best. Share your deepest hurts and frustrations, and your greatest successes and aspirations with God.

*   As soon as you pray to God, start looking for His answer.

*   Trust that God and the universe have the power to produce
     miracles beyond your wildest dreams.

*   Look for the ways in which God does answer your prayers.
     Sometimes it will be in unexpected ways.

TRANSCEND TOXIC
PEOPLE

Father, forgive them; for they know not what they do.

—LUKE 23:34, KJV

* Toxic people fume, rage, lash out at, and manipulate others—not occasionally, as we all do, but habitually and without remorse.

* Encountering a toxic person is like sitting peacefully by the hearth in your own living room when a skunk enters and sprays the whole room. Your peace is destroyed. All you can think

about is how to get rid of the skunk. The best remedy: Get out of the skunk's way. Limit your encounters with toxic people or bring a friend along with you. Surround yourself with supportive people who add to your happiness and self-esteem.

* Toxic people can cause incalculable harm in a family or workplace. If you've grown up with toxic people, you must surround yourself with kind people. It is also crucial to understand that you may feel a perverse attraction to toxic people because of your family history. You may feel urges to engage their angry traits to work out old family business. Resist these urges.

* Stop filling your bucket at a dry well. Would you go to the hardware store to buy oranges? So why should you go to a toxic person for love or support?

* Pray for the offending person. It alleviates your anger.

* Gain some understanding. Most toxic people have survived terrible abuse in their childhoods.

FIND YOUR TRUE VOCATION

Your work is to discover your work and then

with all your heart to give yourself to it.

— BUDDHA

* Select work that you love, that is aligned with your deepest yearnings. Avoid fields that don't deeply interest you. You will be best at what you love. Follow the path that is your heart's deepest desire.

* Persistence and effort are more important than extraordinary talent or genius.

* You must balance idealism with realism. How practical are your dreams? Who else is relying on you? How attainable is your ambition? Pursue your ideal career but also provide for your practical needs.

* Read the best books about how to succeed in your field. Even better, seek out exceptional people in your field. Learn what they did to achieve success.

* Believe that you will succeed. Cultivate determination. And trust that Spirit will guide you.

* When you find your life's work, it will feel not like another road but like a river. You will be flowing downstream, pulled by the current.

5 4

GO ON A RETREAT

Every person needs a retreat, a "dynamo" of silence, where he may go for the

exclusive purpose of being newly recharged by the Infinite.

—PARAMAHANSA YOGANANDA

* Set aside time for relaxation and renewal of spirit.

* Find God in the beauty of nature. Seek out virgin forests, clear
  streams, and awesome mountains.

* Withdrawing from the stress and chaos of daily life can give
  you a whole new perspective on life. On retreat, be open to

intuition and ideas that lead you in new directions. The book you now hold in your hand began while I was on summer retreat at Walden Pond, the refuge of transcendentalist writer Henry David Thoreau.

❋ Take a weekend retreat at home. If you have children, block out time on your calendar to spend alone or with your spouse. Unplug the phone. Bring in flowers. Light candles or incense. Revise your personal mission statement in your journal.

SPREAD KINDNESS

My religion is kindness.

—THE DALAI LAMA

* Once the Dalai Lama, spiritual leader of the Tibetans, was asked, "If someone were to do only one spiritual practice, which one should he choose?" He answered, "Practice kindness."

* Make a list of gifts that you've enjoyed receiving in the past. Each month, select a gift from your list and give it to someone new.

* God embraces us through the love and caring of friendships, for divine love is behind every human love.

* When we give kindness and love, we receive that love reflected back to us.

* Kindness is soul medicine. It revives the weary, and shelters us from the harshness of daily reality.

* Kindness spreads heaven on earth and bridges separation. Giving and receiving kindness joins people together. Each time you ask someone for a favor, it helps create a bond between you. It's understood that you can rely on each other for help, and a blossoming friendship may develop.

LIGHTEN UP

Time spent laughing is time spent with the gods.

—JAPANESE PROVERB

* Look for chances to express humor each day. Find humor in the familiar things of daily life. Laugh and enjoy the present.

* After you've lightened up daily routines, you might stretch yourself. Try a new sport or play a game, like Pictionary, which tests your knowledge or drawing skills. Laugh while you learn.

* Be sociable. People laugh thirty times more often with others than they do alone. Find someone or a group who shares your humor style.

* In India, laughing clubs are popular. Follow their example. Get together with friends to fend off stress with laughing exercises. Be willing to get really silly. Try the Ho-ho, ha-ha exercise used by these clubs. Put your hands in the sky and laugh *Ho-ho, ha-ha, ho-ho, ha-ha* . . .

* The next time you feel a bad mood coming on, smile at once. Maintain a smile for four breaths. This will relax the muscles in your face and lessen irritation. No one can remain in a bad mood when they're smiling.

* Spend time with a young child. A preschooler laughs 400 times a day. The average adult laughs fifteen times a day.

* Place a statue of the laughing Buddha in your home to remind you to emulate God and His sense of humor.

SEEK PEAK EXPERIENCES

"Flow" is . . . the sense of effortless action [people] feel in moments that stand out as the best in their lives. Athletes refer to it as "being in the zone," religious mystics as being in "ecstasy," artists and musicians as aesthetic rapture.

—MIHALY CSIKSZENTMIHALYI

* Do you ever get so absorbed in something that you lose all sense of time? Do you have any work that you would do even if you didn't get paid for it? This is what psychologists call a "flow" experience. The feeling is joyous and fluid because you

are tapping your entire awareness, not merely your conscious perception.

* You can create peak experiences more often by learning the elements of flow. To paraphrase flow expert Dr. Csikszentmihalyi, these elements include:
  — a challenging activity that requires skills within your range
  — an activity that completely absorbs your attention
  — an activity with clear goals and immediate feedback

* Select activities that give rise to flow experiences. Make time for your hobbies. Try things like rock climbing, making music, playing chess, or sailing. Such activities require skills, set up goals, give immediate feedback, and increase the feeling of control.

* Pay attention to the details in your environment. Find ways to set goals in everyday tasks. Set a timer to do housework. Create a decorating or home project. Once we learn the elements of flow, almost any activity can be more fun.

* Life is about rhythm. Happy lives have a deep sense of rhythm filled with many flow experiences. Unhappy lives have little sense of rhythm.

MAKE YOUR HOME
A REFUGE

Wherever you live is your temple if you treat it like one.

—JACK KORNFIELD

* Make your house a sacred space, a place of refuge, where you can deeply relax.

* Arrange a special place in your home where you can pray and meditate every day.

* Fill your house with paintings, flowers, music, and your favorite scents.

* Place warm colors and good lighting throughout your home. Intersperse small lamps with overhead lighting to create warm pools of light. Good lighting has an enormous effect on mood.

DESIGN YOUR OWN MAP

There is more happiness in doing one's own [path] without excellence than

in doing another's [path] well. It is happier to die in one's own law;

another's [path] brings dread.

—THE BHAGAVAD GITA 3:35

* Don't be afraid to create your own personal religion. More than 100 years ago, William James, author of the classic *Varieties of Religious Experience*, described his religion as "piecemealed." Build your own spiritual life from a mosaic of beliefs. Find teachings that excite you or fill you with wonder.

* Explore different religions. Take what you need and leave the rest. Bringing back ideas from other religions can revitalize or update your own religion and help it address your real needs. Other teachers can even help you discover the jewels in your own tradition.

* Share stories with others about your spiritual journeys. You'll be amazed at how many people feel they don't "fit in" to organized religion, yet deeply want spirituality in their lives.

* Form your own spirituality group with friends. Find a spiritual buddy to meet with weekly for encouragement. Read and discuss a specific spiritual book.

* Keep connected. Search the Web for new groups. Go to conferences or lectures. Attend spiritual ceremonies.

* Do you feel uprooted sometimes for having left a religious group? Do you miss a group that you once loved? If you join a group and later discover that you don't fit in, you have options. You can find a new group, piecemeal your own religion, or remain involved but focus only on the group's best values.

60

WALK TO MEDITATE

When we walk like [we are running], we print anxiety and sorrow on the

Earth. We have to walk in a way that we only print peace and serenity on

the Earth . . . Be aware of the contact between your feet and the Earth.

Walk as if you are kissing the Earth with your feet.

—THICH NHAT HANH

* Sometimes we are too agitated to sit and meditate. Walking
  meditation can work beautifully as well.

* There are many ways to practice walking meditation. As you breathe in, silently count your steps, "One, two, three." As you breathe out, count "One, two, three." Or as you walk, you can recite a focus word, like "peace" or "love."

* As you focus on the physical act of walking and breathing for twenty to thirty minutes, your mind becomes peaceful and relaxed. You let go of anger and get in touch with the present moment.

* As you walk, take in the beauty of nature. Take time to look at the oak and maple trees, the dogwood trees and hibiscus flowers, and the changing colors of the sky.

* Walk slowly. Be aware of every step of lifting and placing your feet. Focus on your breathing and body movements. Relax, take off your shoes, wiggle your toes, and feel the earth.

* Go for a walking meditation along the beach. Walk in the wet dark sand down by the ocean and in the high white sand up by the dunes. Give every sensation its full value.

* You might try reciting a verse while you walk, such as this one written by Thich Nhat Hanh:

I have arrived.
I am home.
In the here,
In the now.
I am solid.
I am free.
In the ultimate
I dwell.

6 1

PRACTICE YOGA

Even a little practice of this Yoga delivers one from great fear.

— THE BHAGAVAD GITA 2:40

* The Bhagavad Gita claims that yoga is among the highest methods ever given to humankind by God for achieving union with the Infinite.

* Yoga means "union." Yoga is a system of ancient techniques designed to raise one's consciousness to achieve union with God. Yoga's purpose is divine—to unite the body with the soul. It does this by switching off the mind and life energy

from the senses and turning the energy inward toward the Infinite.

* Use yoga to carve out sacred time each day to rest and relax.

* Learn yoga to deeply relax, unwind at the end of a hectic day, and eliminate fear.

LEARN THE SECRET TO SUCCESS

Success is preparation meeting timing.

—AMERICAN PROVERB

* The secret to success is to believe that you will succeed. Know that God is protecting and guiding you.

* In *How to Be Rich*, oil tycoon and author J. Paul Getty tells us that he failed more than the average person. The main difference between him and the average person was that he kept trying and never gave up.

* You do not need to possess extraordinary talent to succeed, but you do need to discover work that you love and, then, persist until you succeed.

* Mingle with successful people. Learn how they got where they are. Model your efforts after theirs.

* Plant thoughts of success in your subconscious mind. When you speak aloud, never put yourself down or doubt your success.

* Keep a monthly record of your successes. Say "thank you" for each of them. You will attract more success.

* If success eludes you, consider that you may be in the wrong line of work. Pay attention to the kind of work that makes your heart soar, for this is the very work you will thrive at.

* When you discover work you love, persist in taking action steps until you succeed. After many years of trying, one day you will wake up and, suddenly, success will be yours.

6 3

CREATE AND SAVOR

RITUALS

Ritual is the way we carry the presence of the sacred.

Ritual is the spark that must not go out.

—CHRISTINA BALDWIN

* Rituals slow down the hectic pace of daily life. Escape the rat race of everyday life by creating your own rituals. Set aside time to pray and meditate. Light incense or candles. Sound a meditation bell. Find some literature that inspires you and read it every day.

* Develop favorite Sunday routines and activities. Try playing tennis or bridge with a friend.

* Create your own rituals. Invite friends over for dinner or Scrabble each month. Create annual family or holiday rituals that you'll look forward to each year. Try a monthly creative excursion: visit a museum, a fabric store, an art-supply store. Attend a lecture, buy theater tickets, or browse in a bookstore.

* Replenish yourself with physical rituals: get a facial or a full-body massage. Relax in a steamy whirlpool surrounded by eucalyptus plants.

* Work rituals are practical tasks that have functional use and some aesthetic merit. Some people enjoy handwashing dishes, sorting or folding laundry, or polishing silver.

* Ritual is most important in the tough times. Do not put off celebrating a ritual because you don't "feel up to it." Ritual should be restorative. It's no accident that Christmas comes in the darkest week of the year.

* Rituals should never be done by rote. Work to keep your ritual fresh and new.

6 4

FIND YOUR CENTER

. . . behold, the kingdom of God is within you.

LUKE 17:21, KJV

* Enlightened ones in all nations throughout history have taught that everything we're searching for lies within. Within is a doorway to the soul. Vedic scriptures say "Thou art That," or "You are Spirit."

* Take time to slow down. Let quiet envelop you. Find your center. Meditate.

* Just ten minutes a day of meditation can elicit a deep state of

relaxation, create mindful breathing that stills the riled soul, and bolster the immune system.

* Never underestimate how deeply the subconscious acts on our lives. Explore deep-seated beliefs that are holding you back or keeping you from seeing your own power. Replace limiting beliefs with more positive thoughts.

* We are incredibly powerful beings, but our power is within us. Only by going within can we begin to tap that power. Don't make other people's opinions more important than your own. Never assume that all the answers are outside yourself. The answers are probably within.

* Realize that our experiences are a reflection of our inner psychological state. If we locate the kingdom of heaven within, we can experience the kingdom of heaven on earth.

CREATE PROSPERITY

Money will come when you are doing the right thing.

— MIKE PHILLIPS

* Our culture often implies that money and material possession are in conflict with spiritual life. People take literally the symbolic words of Jesus: "It is harder for a rich man to get into heaven than for a camel to go through the eye of a needle." But this isn't always true.

* Tune in to God's infinite abundance. In prayer or meditation, establish contact with God and affirm, "I am open and ready

to receive the good that is now mine," or "All things whatsoever the Father hath are mine."

* Now, work to become prosperous. Affirming abundance on its own won't bring money. You must couple work and action with affirmation and prayer.

* Find work that you love, that you will do gladly and joyously. Now persevere in that work and you will prosper.

* Realize that negative thoughts, such as fear and worry, weaken the flow of abundance while gratitude and praise expand your consciousness and create more prosperity.

* Generosity also attracts further prosperity. Use your money to help others and you'll create more happiness in your own heart, too.

PART THREE

MAPS
FOR THE
SOUL

66

FOLLOW YOUR BLISS

I say follow your bliss and don't be afraid, and doors will

open where you didn't know they were going to be.

—JOSEPH CAMPBELL

* The single most important piece of advice I can give you for your journey is to follow your bliss.

* Keep trying different things until you discover what you love doing. Then go after it with all your heart.

* First, you may only be able to do what you love for one hour a day while you earn your livelihood. But if you follow your

heart, unimaginable doors will open for you. Abundance and joy beyond your wildest imagination will be yours.

* "Follow your bliss and doors will open" is a universal truth and, as such, it cannot fail. Follow your intuitions of where your bliss is. Pursue your inner inclinations and unfinished dreams.

INVITE AN ANGEL
INTO YOUR LIFE

I am going to send an angel in front of you, to guard you on the way . . .

Be attentive to him and listen to his voice . . . for my name is in him.

—EXODUS 23:20–21, NEW REVISED STANDARD
VERSION (NRSV)

The angels love our tears . . . Leaving, they dry our face with the brush

of a wing, never seeing it pure . . . already far away from us . . .

—RAINER MARIA RILKE

* As soon as a child cries, an angel comes and sits upon his shoulder.

* You may be wondering, "Where is my angel?" Your angel may be right in front of you. Your best friend may be an angel sent to you by God.

* Invite an angel into your life and allow her to guide you to safety. Look for your angel's message to come through your heart's sense of inner knowing. Angels touch us through writing, meditation, the kindness of strangers, or words of wisdom spoken by a friend.

* After you've met your angel, it's not enough to sit back. Ask yourself, "Whose angel can I become today?" Bring a child a surprise present, visit a sick relative, give someone a compliment, or call a friend who's going through a hard time.

ASK GOD FOR HELP

Ask, and it shall be given you; seek, and ye shall find; knock,

and it shall be opened unto you.

MATTHEW 7:7, KJV

* Ask God for help and believe you will receive it.

* All day watch for signs that a Higher Power is helping you.

* Say "Thank you" for the help when it arrives.

* Accept the fact that you don't have to do everything alone. Ask for help from friends, mentors, or a Higher Power. Let God's love flow to you through the helping hands of others.

* When you ask for help, you become open to receiving God's abundance.

* Asking for help connects you with others and gives them permission to accept help as well.

* Believe that you are worthy to receive help.

WATCH FOR SIGNS
AND WONDERS

God Himself does not speak prose, but

communicates with us by hints, [signs],

inferences and . . . objects lying all around us.

—RALPH WALDO EMERSON

*   Make a daily "signs and wonders" list, a list of signs or evidence that God is helping you. Note a lovely sunset, or a letter bearing good news from an old friend.

* When you're feeling blue, reread old lists to see how Spirit has helped you before. Be assured that God will help you again.

* Open the Bible to a random page and study the first verse that catches your eye.

* Even in your darkest hour, help will come to you from an unexpected source. Have faith.

GIVE YOUR LIFE THE HIGHEST VISION

Dream lofty dreams, and as you dream, so shall you become.
Your vision is the promise of what you shall one day be; your ideal
is the prophecy of what you shall at last unveil.

—JAMES ALLEN

* Commit to living the highest vision for your life, and prosperity,
joy, and love beyond your wildest dreams will be realized.

* When you follow your dreams, you connect to a wellspring of healing and happiness. Unite your life with Spirit by living the highest vision for your life.

* God is joy and ever-new bliss, so when you live in joy, you are living in God. When you follow your dreams, you are refreshed and renewed by Spirit each day.

* Ask yourself, "What is standing between me and the vision I have for my life?" Use willpower to drop the beliefs that hold you back. You have the power to choose and live your life according to new beliefs.

* The only limitations are the ones you place on yourself.

MAKE A CONNECTION

For where two or three are gathered together in my name,

there am I in the midst of them.

—MATTHEW 18:20, KJV

. . . your whole life is composed by the will within you. And just as people

whom you will have met apparently by mere chance became leading agents in

the structuring of your life, so, too, will you have served unknowingly as an

agent, giving meaning to the lives of others.

—JOSEPH CAMPBELL

* Disconnection is an illusion. Souls know nothing of separation.

* Devote time every day to a goal or project larger than yourself.

* Start a project in your life, and one that contains within it a series of goals. Projects give order and meaning to our lives. They allow us to achieve our goals in a planned sequence.

* Schedule time each day to make a connection with yourself. Be still, light incense, exercise, or write in your journal. Be present so that you can feel the inner presence of the Divine within.

* Draw up a list entitled "Connections." Write down the names and phone numbers of friends, acquaintances, potential friends, meaningful activities, and spiritual practices you can summon whenever you need to reconnect.

72

SAVOR SPIRITUAL

FRIENDSHIPS

It is God who comes to you in the guise of a true and noble friend

to serve, inspire, and guide you.

—PARAMAHANSA YOGANANDA

* To have friends, manifest friendliness.

* Offer your friends good cheer in times of struggle, heartbreak, and distress.

* Encourage and inspire your friends.

*   Be full of compassion.

*   Rejoice in your friends' good fortune.

*   Rid yourself of jealousy, which poisons friendship.

NOURISH YOUR RELATIONSHIPS

The Holy Spirit's temple is not a body, but a relationship.

— *A COURSE IN MIRACLES*

* Look for the divinity in everyone you encounter: letter carriers, flight attendants, grocery clerks.

* Listen to your friends. Volunteer to help them. The deeper the mutual support, the deeper the friendship.

* Accept the fact that people can only change so much. See the whole person. Release your judgments and focus on people's positive traits.

* Touch those you love. Put your arms around them. Make sure they know you love them.

* We've all had the experience of feeling instantly drawn to certain people. Cherish those times. You may have known that person in another lifetime.

* Look for love in your relationships. Focus on what you're getting rather than what you're missing. Every relationship can teach us something. When relationships are hard or painful, ask yourself, "What can this relationship teach me?"

* At the end of our lives, what we and others will remember most is the quality of our relationships. How well did we love?

* Listen. Listening sounds simple, but it is not. The more interest you show in other people, the more interest they will show in you.

CALL GOD TO YOU

Call unto me, and I will answer thee, and show

thee great and mighty things, which thou knowest not.

—JEREMIAH 33:3, KJV

* Remind yourself that there is no separation between you and God.

* Write a heartfelt letter to God, meditate, or create a sacred space.

* Make a God box. Get a decorative box or container. Place a picture of your favorite saint on the top. Get out a piece of

paper. Write down a prayer request and place it in the box. Once you place your problem in the box, surrender the problem to Spirit, trusting that Spirit will guide you to a solution.

* You asked God for something and put the prayer request in your God box. Now six months have passed and God hasn't answered. Tear up the request and write a new one. Your needs may have changed since you wrote the old request. Taking this kind of action gathers new energy for your request and restores your faith that your prayer will be answered.

KNOW THAT LOVE
WAITS FOR YOU

There were times you did not succeed.

Walking on the empty path, you were floating in the air,

lost in the cycle of birth and death

and drawn into the world of illusion.

But the beautiful path is patient,

always waiting for you to come back,

that path that is so familiar to you,

and so faithful.

It knows you will come back one day.

And it will welcome you back.

The path will be as fresh and as beautiful as the first time.

Love never says that this is the last time.

—THICH NHAT HANH

* If you feel far from any sense of divine mystery, begin where you are: say a simple prayer, light a candle, meditate for two minutes. It doesn't take much. Love always welcomes you back.

* Muslims say if you take one step toward Allah, He takes two steps toward you.

76

KNOW THAT YOU
ARE NEVER ALONE

I am not alone.

He that sent me is with me.

I and my Father are one.

—JESUS IN JOHN 8:16, 8:29, AND 10:30, KJV

* Jesus knew that God was with him, and he left a beautiful testimony to that sacred knowledge.

* Believe that you, too, have a Divine Partner to walk with you through life.

* Whenever you face turmoil or stormy weather, take your Higher Power with you.

* Just as the little wave is never separate from the ocean, our soul is never separate from God. The Bhagavad Gita says, "Thou art That"—that the indwelling spirit (the atman) is the same as God or Brahman. So there exists utter union between God and human beings. Buddhists say that all beings have Buddha nature.

* Never doubt that you are supported by a loving presence.

* Develop the habit of mentally whispering to God. Cultivate the feeling that God is by your side and that you are backed by a helping power.

77

FIND COMMUNITY

To be rooted is perhaps the most important

and least recognized

need of the human soul.

—SIMONE WEIL

*　Make your own community of just two or three. Start a spiritual reading group with friends. Create a sacred circle to nourish your spiritual practice. God will be there in your living room fellowship as much as He is present in a large church gathering.

* Realize that if you are searching for God by developing your own personal religion, you are a courageous member of a growing community that is millions strong.

* Don't expect any one group to be perfect. Find the best community you can and savor its jewels and wisdom.

FIND HEAVEN WITHIN

The kingdom of heaven is spread out upon the earth,

and people do not see it.

—THOMAS 113:4, SV

* We create heaven and hell through our own thoughts and behavior.

* Heaven is a psychological state of peace and joy within. Develop and follow psychological and spiritual disciplines so that you can find heaven in this lifetime.

* When we follow our bliss, we connect to the Spirit and to love, and, in the words of St. Catherine, "All the way to heaven is heaven."

* Never allow yourself to think like a victim, and you can create heaven within.

NOURISH YOUR SOUL

WITH MUSIC

After silence that which comes nearest to expressing

the inexpressible is music.

—ALDOUS HUXLEY

* Music affects the body, which in turn affects the mind and
soul. Music has long been related to the spirit. The sacred
music of other cultures moves us even if we have never heard it
before. The haunting sounds of Gregorian chants and the other-
worldly sounds of Tibetans chanting the om vibration stir our

deepest emotions and uplift our consciousness from the mundane to the sacred.

* Music relaxes us. Just as you may read spiritual literature each day for nourishment, listen to harmonious music each day to fend off stress, rejuvenate yourself, and uplift your mood. See if you don't feel more relaxed at the end of the day.

* Music sanctifies daily life. Browse in a New Age gift store for soothing music to add to your collection.

* Music heals us. Listening to peaceful music lowers heart rate, reduces stress and fear, and increases deep relaxation.

* Explore these sacred and soothing sounds: Albinoni's *Adagio for Strings, Piano Reflections* by Kelly Yost (Channel Productions), *Chant* by the Benedictine Monks of Santo Domingo De Silos (Angel Records), *Vision: The Music of Hildegard von Bingen* (Angel Records), *Invocation: Sacred Music from Around the World* (Music of the World).

GIVE THANKS TO A HIGHER POWER

If thank you is the only prayer you say, that will be enough.

— MEISTER ECKHART

* Just as you would thank a friend who helped you, thank God, your friend of all friends, for all the blessings in your life.

* The more you give thanks to Spirit, the more blessings will come to you.

* Make each entry in your gratitude journal a prayer or thank you to the universe.

* God wants to give you everything. How wide can you open your arms, heart, and mind to receive?

* Praise is a reverent thank you to God. Praise is a choice you make to find something good about life. Praise develops gratitude, gratitude leads to love, and love leads to compassion.

* Offering praise heals the stress in our lives. Each day find five things to praise. You might thank God for the trees, the rain, the flowers, and the sunlight. But save at least one bit of praise for a human being who needs it.

TALK WITH GOD

The call does not come to the ear, but to the heart.

One does not hear *it as much as he* knows *it.*

—FULTON J. SHEEN

* Again and again, the Scriptures reveal communication between God and people. God speaks to us through intuition, through dreams, through a deep sense of inner knowing.

* Although the outward paths of each religion are different, every religion teaches us that we must speak to God from our hearts.

* It's easier to communicate if you have a personal conception of God. Think of God as Friend, Companion, or Beloved.

*   Approach God with gratitude and devotion. These attitudes attract God's response.

*   Be open to your intuition. Become receptive to Spirit's guidance.

*   Cultivate the feeling that God is close and near. Pray and know that God will answer. Be persistent in your communication and you will receive help.

LISTEN DEEPLY

I vow to cultivate loving speech and deep listening in order to bring joy

and happiness to others and to relieve them of their suffering.

—THICH NHAT HANH

* To help ease a person's suffering, practice deep listening.

* Be fully present. Pay attention. Look into people's eyes, nod your head, say little or nothing. Release judgments about what you are hearing. Calm down your "inner chatter" or plan of how you'll respond.

* Listen for the feelings behind the person's words. Occasionally, mirror back what you are hearing.

* Cultivate compassion for yourself and others. While someone speaks, mentally send a loving-kindness phrase like, "May you be well." You'll be amazed at the powerful effect this has on the interaction.

* Alleviate your suffering so that you can better listen to and love others.

WRITE A LETTER
TO GOD

God talks to His devotees through intuitive feeling, through friends,

through light-writing, and through a Voice heard within.

—PARAMAHANSA YOGANANDA

* Have you ever read something whose words seemed to jump off the page? Be alert to Spirit's messages that come through writing.

* Write a heartfelt letter to God. Begin a journal entry with the words, "Dear God." Tell God your deepest hurts and most

cherished desires. Pour out all of your hardships, the I-can't-take-it-anymore feelings. Give your problem to God and be alert to ways throughout the day that the Spirit helps you.

* Place affirmations or prayer requests in your God box.

* Write a question in your journal. Then write down what God's response might be.

SING TO GOD

One who sings to God prays twice.

—ST. AMBROSE

* Devotional music gives voice to our spirits. Throughout the
   ages, it has been used to elicit God's response. Chants, or spiritual songs, that have been written and spiritualized by great
   masters, when sung with devotion, can lift our consciousness to
   the transcendent.

* Spiritual music expresses the soul's deep longing for divine love.

* Awaken devotion. Sing or listen to sacred chants. Seek the meaning behind the words.

* Sing with devotion, alone or in a group, and you will begin to feel the power of the transcendent. You will be showered with blessings.

* Build a sacred music library. Discover favorite devotional music that can soothe and comfort you.

* If you lose a loved one, listen to a sacred chant. Focus all of your heart on the soul of your loved one. Listen to the chant until you feel the soul ascending to realms of light. Feel the joy that the soul now feels. The joyous feelings that the chant awakens are a sign of God's presence. Know that your loved one dwells in the Divine.

* Cherish other sounds that touch the spirit: rainfall on rooftops, wind chimes, ocean waves breaking on the shore.

CRAVE GOD

Be filled with one wish, for God, God, God.

Unless you are single-hearted, my dears,

He is very hard to find.

— SRI DAYA MATA

* Put your spiritual life first, and everything else will fall into place.

* Any relationship takes cultivation, time, and desire. The same is true for your relationship with God. Cultivate the relationship

in good times. It will be so much easier to find God in difficult moments.

* If you don't crave God, crave one of God's forms, such as Creativity, Beauty, Nature, or Love—whatever quality you most want to infuse your life with.

8 6

LEARN LOVE
MEDITATION

May I be peaceful and happy.

May I be safe and free from injury.

May I be free from anger, fear, and anxiety.

—BUDDHIST MEDITATION VERSES

*   In Buddhism, there is a spiritual practice called "love meditation" or the practice of loving-kindness. Love meditation is a
powerful tool for bringing love to yourself and sending it to

others. You can recite the above phrases while sitting in meditation or mentally during daily activity.

* In sitting meditation, repeat the phrases to yourself for five to ten minutes. Try to feel friendship and love for yourself. Become aware of how you are treating yourself—your body, thoughts, and feelings.

* After you have sent the phrases to yourself, send them to someone you like, then to a neutral person, and finally to an enemy or former tormentor. When you say the phrases, bring the image of the person into your mind—how he looks, talks, and walks. When we contemplate our enemy's suffering, we generate understanding, which dissolves the anger and hatred within us.

* Cultivate compassion and love for yourself. Then give that love to others. If you practice love meditation, you will learn the art of bringing forth love in the present moment. You will feel happier and more peaceful.

87

WATCH FOR SAINTS

To encounter a true master is worth a century of studying

his or her teaching . . . How can we encounter a true master?

It depends on us. Many who looked directly into the eyes of the Buddha

or the eyes of Jesus were not capable of seeing them.

—THICH NHAT HANH

* Saints' lives represent the fruits of religion—inward tranquility, belief in a divine order, tangible safety, and a sense of wonder. They also embody God's immense love for us.

* Know that God sends his saints and avatars, divine incarnations of Him, in every age to ease our suffering.

* A saint can also initiate us into all the mystic teachings and stimulate our desire for enlightenment.

* Attend lectures or retreats where saints will be. Bring home videos or tapes by them to inspire you.

* Fill your mind with the qualities of your saint—deep respect for the way they treat others, compassion, humor, or commitment to meditation.

* Read about the lives of great saints. Study their teachings. Live in their world of miracles, signs, and wonders.

8 8

GIVE SERVICE

The fruit of love is service, which is compassion in action.

— MOTHER TERESA

The more we take the welfare of others to heart and work for their benefit,

the more benefit we derive for ourselves. This is a fact that we can see.

— THE DALAI LAMA

* Reflect about your own life and how much difference one indi-
vidual has made for you. Realize that you can make the same
difference in someone else's life.

* Look for ways to serve those around you: acquaintances, coworkers, family members, and friends.

* Service might include deep listening, calling a friend with encouragement, praying for others, or taking a child from a troubled home under your wing.

* Find a way without words to show someone you care.

* The next time a friend is late for an appointment with you, pray for him while you wait. It's hard to resent someone for whom you pray.

* Giving is the right thing to do. Giving comes back to us. The more you give to others, the more you will receive.

LOVE

That Love is all there is,

Is all we know of Love

—EMILY DICKINSON

It is not a matter of thinking a great deal but of loving a great deal,

so do whatever arouses you most to love.

—ST. TERESA OF AVILA

* Scriptures and saints from all ages and religions tell us that
God is love.

* Love is the infinite self made visible. When we love, we are closest to the Divine. Vow to create more love in all areas of your life—work, home, friendships, hobbies, choice of a life partner.

* Love attracts love. The love we give out returns to us multiplied. The love that we feel for others is a reflection of the love at the seat of our being. We may think that we love another person because of who they are and what they have done. But, in fact, we love because it is the nature of our being.

* God loves everyone unconditionally.

* Cultivate love. A heart filled with love is a healing, life-changing force. Love can heal all wounds.

* Love never dies. All the feelings of love we have ever felt are being stored up for us, and when we die, we will be reunited with all this love and more.

* Love survives the death of dear ones. Our love for the living and departed creates eternal bonds that are with us through many lifetimes.

REIMAGINE GOD

One may visualize God in whatever aspect rouses one's devotion

and keeps his mind inwardly attuned to the Divine.

—SRI DAYA MATA

* Develop a personal conception of God. Try to feel an intimate relationship with Him. You might think of God as Divine Mother, as Love, as Jesus, as Buddha, or whatever image inspires you.

* Do not fear that adapting religion is somehow sacrilegious. Religious reform can be seen in the light of adaptation.

* Create an image of God that affirms your authentic self, incorporates your qualities, and understands and celebrates your difference. The Bhagavad Gita says that God's manifestations are infinite.

* Adapt your conception of God. Does your religion bring happiness, peace, and love to your everyday life? What is your vision of spirituality? How have you been damaged by a patriarchal, judging God?

* Envision a God who will hold your interest. If our vision of God includes bliss, then we have a reason to seek God and to find ways to weave the Spirit into our everyday search for happiness.

MEDITATE

There is nothing in all creation so like God as stillness.

—MEISTER ECKHART

* Meditation is a form of concentration. We attune ourselves to the power of Spirit. We meet God at the altar of the silence of our soul.

* Meditation occurs whenever we are fully absorbed in the present moment. Any activity can be a meditation to awaken to wonder and life.

* Make meditation a habit. Meditate for at least five minutes each day. The more you meditate, the greater your desire will be to do it again.

* Use meditation to relax deeply. Just ten minutes of meditation can elicit the "relaxation response," a deep state of relaxation, which scientists have found boosts the immune system and significantly reduces stress.

* Set aside a small meditation room or corner of a room. Make its atmosphere conducive to meditation. Place incense there, a candle, a picture of your favorite teacher. Create a sanctuary where you can rejuvenate, relax, or connect with peace.

* When you meditate, affirm and visualize your ideal life. This sows seeds of success in your subconscious mind, which then act to make the thought real.

* Pray to God from the silent peace of meditation. Prayers offered to God from meditation are especially powerful.

HAVE COMPASSION

FOR OTHERS

If we could read the secret history of our enemies,

we should find in each man's life sorrow and

suffering enough to disarm all hostility.

—HENRY WADSWORTH LONGFELLOW

* Pity the person who harms you. Pray for the person who angers you. Imagine how much pain they must feel to treat you this way.

*   If someone's ignorance or greed has hurt you, remember that, although it may take years, truth always prevails in the end.

*   Meditate. Envision your enemy as a wounded five-year-old child. Tell him or her, "I forgive you, and I let you go."

KNOW THAT LOVE
SURVIVES DEATH

When you lose a dear one, meditate . . . then put your mind on the

one you have lost. Visualize him and mentally send him your love,

again and again. The vibration of love reaches out beyond this

finite world and touches that soul, wherever he is.

—SRI DAYA MATA

* Think of death as a crossing to the other side. Our loved ones
find ecstasy when they are taken home to God. As their souls

ascend to Spirit, they cross over to a state of bliss, light, and boundless love.

* Never lose faith that you will see your deceased loved ones again.

* Our departed loved ones touch us through dreams. They are telling us, "I love you. I miss you. I'm still around. I'm still looking in on you."

* Our departed loved ones live on in the thoughts and actions of their families—in the shape of their bodies, eyes, words, and hearts. The love of one grandmother, after she's gone, can transform her daughter, who can then transform the grand-daughter. One heart, anchored in divine love, can hold a whole family in the light.

HEAL YOUR HEARTACHES

How poor are they that have not patience!

What wound did ever heal but by degrees?

—IAGO, *OTHELLO*

* Make a plan for your own healing. Write down the phone numbers of friends to call for support, new activities to try, favorite distractions, good books to read or videos to rent. Gather affirmations and powerful quotations. Replace thoughts of failure or lacking with your favorite thoughts on success and prosperity.

* Know that you will survive. Indeed, you will do better than that: You will fall in love again. Remember that this, too, shall pass.

* Grieving the loss of a lover is like putting alcohol on a wound—painful in the short term but good for you in the long term. The pain from ending a bad relationship can seem endless. When leaving is sure to bring pain, we are loathe to leave. But sometimes we must leave, and bear the pain, for the sake of our future.

* Every day try to expand your compassion for yourself a little further. If your lover has rejected you, don't reject or abandon yourself. Give yourself the caring and compassion you wanted from a partner.

* When relationships fail, be honest about why. Solicit constructive criticism from your lover, your best friend, your counselor—and then vow to not make the same mistakes again.

* Focus not on what you are leaving behind but on what you are reaching for—a healthy relationship with someone who can meet most of your needs.

FORGIVE OTHERS

All have their frailties and whoever looks for a friend

without imperfections will never find what he seeks.

—CYRUS THE GREAT

* Pray for the person who hurts you. Release the person with love and forgiveness and you are free.

* When you feel that someone has hurt you too much to forgive, sit in meditation. Say the words, "I forgive you," and "I let you go." You don't have to feel forgiveness in your heart in order to say the words. Saying the words, even when you don't feel them, frees you from anger, pain, and a sense of yourself as a victim.

* Forgiveness is as much for you as it is for the other person. Forgiveness is a gift that you give yourself.

* Trust your conscience to tell you when you need to make amends.

* Don't rush forgiveness. It will come on its own accord, sometimes only at the end of a long healing process. You can only forgive someone after you have had enough love and compassion to treat your own hurt.

SURRENDER YOUR PROBLEM
TO A HIGHER POWER

We must stop planning, plotting, and scheming and let

Infinite Intelligence solve the problem in Its own way . . .

Our part is to prepare for our blessings and

follow our intuitive leads.

—FLORENCE SCOVEL SHINN

* Place your life in God's hands and trust that there is a divine plan.

* God never makes you change without making sure that you have all the help you need.

* Don't struggle too much with trying to figure out solutions to difficult problems. When you put your life in God's hands, you relax your mind. New solutions will come to you.

* Keep turning to God and you will be calmer, more serene. Your intuition will tell you what to do.

* Use the prayer, "Thy will, not mine, be done."

* Surrendering your problem to a Higher Power doesn't mean that you stop taking action. It simply means that you do everything you can and then trust that a Higher Power will make everything work out for the best.

PREPARE FOR ETERNITY

To see a world in a grain of sand,

And a heaven in a wild flower,

Hold infinity in the palm of your hand,

And eternity in an hour.

—WILLIAM BLAKE

* The scriptures of India say that in God's consciousness the past, present, and future dissolve into an eternal Now and that the soul of a person is immortal.

* We've all experienced glimpses of eternity, synchronistic

moments when time seems to stand still. The Buddha taught that if we look deeply, we will see that the present is made from the past and the future is made from the present.

* Savor the time you spend with loved ones. You can never tell them "I love you" too much. Then when you or they pass away, you'll have no regrets. Your loved ones will be comforted by how much you loved them.

* People die as they have lived. If your life has been filled with radiance and love, you will view death as a peaceful and transcendent experience. This peace will enter into the hearts of your loved ones as you pass away and will be a great comfort to them after you're gone.

* When my grandmother, a great devotee of Jesus, was dying, my mother placed an angel pin on her hospital gown. It helped my family to focus on the ascension of her Spirit and on what an angel she had truly been to all of us.

* When a loved one is dying, surround her bedside. Pour out your love for her. Let the love envelop you both. Feel her Spirit ascending to the Great Spirit, the heavenly realm of love and pure bliss.

98

RECOGNIZE TEACHERS

When the student is ready, the Master appears.

—BUDDHIST PROVERB

* As soon as a soul yearns for help, God sends help in the form of a teacher or enlightened one.

* Find a teacher who can help you unlock an experience of illumination. The Bhagavad Gita tells us that God determines in advance each person's teachers or gurus. Many people report that when they first met their guru or found the right spiritual path, they felt an instant and powerful feeling of having come home.

* Teachers can be mentors, saints, books, or vivid experiences, like a difficult relationship or an encounter with death.

* When in the presence of an enlightened person, be open and receive from his consciousness. Keep it simple.

* The Buddha advised us to never get too attached to any one teacher or religion. He said, "Be lamps unto yourselves. Be a refuge unto yourselves."

KNOW THAT GOD WORKS
THROUGH OTHERS

Coincidences are God's way of remaining anonymous.

—FRENCH PROVERB

* Divine love is the source behind all human love.

* God speaks through:
  — coincidence
  — a friend's love, compassion, and encouragement
  — the discovery of a new spiritual path
  — the job offer that comes when you may desperately need
    some money

— a personal story of pain and triumph that rekindles hope or leads you to an important answer
— a friend's words of wisdom that bring a message you need on your journey
— miracles

* God works through people. Through others, he sends hugs, love, support, and hears our personal stories of pain and triumph. Find a group where you can connect with many people and meet regularly with God.

* Miracles are God's way of saying, "I am with you. I will make the way safe for you. I have heard every cry from your heart. I send you a miracle out of my compassion and love for you."

TRUST

. . . with God all things are possible.

—MARK 10:27

There is a soul force in the universe, which, if we permit it,

will flow through us and produce miraculous results.

—MAHATMA GANDHI

* Trust that there is a divine plan working in your life.

* Practice trust. Choose a stressful situation, and just for one day, trust that everything will turn out okay. Notice how this affects your mood throughout the day.

* Reflect on the times when you didn't know how you would get through. Didn't a blessing suddenly come from out of the blue? Know that there will always be "helping hands" and blessings to guide you to safety. But you must have faith that they are there.

* Beware of jumping to negative conclusions about the future. We just don't know how the future is going to turn out.

* Ask a Higher Power for help in all areas—money, relationships, career. Scientists have found that faith reduces stress and preserves your health. An attitude of trust frees up energy to find new solutions to problems.

* Has your trust been broken by other people or by God? That's okay. It's human to doubt sometimes. The best thing you can do in a crisis of faith is to relax and ride it out. Your ability to trust will return. Ask God to help you with trust, to send reliable people into your life who will help heal your trust issues. Discover how easy it is to trust when you fill your life with trustworthy people.

S U G G E S T E D
R E A D I N G

Bloomfield, Harold; and McWilliams, Peter. *How to Heal Depression*. Los Angeles: Prelude Press, 1994.

Burns, David. *Feeling Good*. New York: William Morrow and Company, Inc., 1980.

Campbell, Joseph. *The Power of Myth*. New York: Doubleday, 1988.

Colgrove, Melba; Bloomfield, Harold; and McWilliams, Peter. *How to Survive the Loss of a Love*. Los Angeles: Prelude Press, 1976.

Covey, Stephen R. *The Seven Habits of Highly Effective People*. New York: Simon & Schuster, 1990.

Csikszentmihalyi, Mihaly. *Flow: The Psychology of Optimal Experience*. New York: HarperCollins, 1990.

Frankl, Viktor E. *Man's Search for Meaning*. Boston: Beacon Press, 1963.

Hanh, Thich Nhat. *Living Buddha, Living Christ*. New York: G.P. Putnam's Sons, 1995.

————. *Teachings on Love*. Berkeley, California: Parallax Press, 1997.

————. *Touching Peace.* Berkeley, California: Parallax Press, 1992.

Hendrix, Harville. *Keeping the Love You Find.* New York: Simon & Schuster, 1992.

Holmes, Ernest. *Creative Mind and Success.* New York: R.M. McBride, 1919.

————. *The Science of Mind.* New York: R.M. McBride, 1938.

James, William. *The Varieties of Religious Experience.* USA: Longmans, Green, and Co., 1902. Reprinted in New York: Penguin Books, 1982.

Johnson, Spencer. *Yes or No: The Guide to Better Decisions.* New York: HarperCollins, 1992.

Kiersey, David; and Bates, Marilyn. *Please Understand Me.* Del Mar, California: Promethean Nemesis, 1984.

Kornfield, Jack. *A Path with Heart.* New York: Bantam, 1993.

Krishnamurti, J. *On Fear.* New York: HarperCollins, 1995.

Pagels, Elaine. *The Gnostic Gospels.* New York: Random House, 1979.

Rahula, Walpola. *What the Buddha Taught.* Bedford, England: G. Fraser, 1959. Revised edition published in New York: Random House, 1974.

Robinson, James M. *The Nag Hammadi Library.* New York: Harper & Row, 1977.

Salzberg, Sharon. *Lovingkindness*. Boston: Shambhala, 1995.

Vaughan, Frances; and Walsh, Roger, eds. *Gifts From a Course in Miracles*. New York: G.P. Putnam's Sons, 1995.

Yogananda, Paramahansa. *The Divine Romance*. Los Angeles: Self-Realization Fellowship, 1986.

S O U R C E S

Allen, James. *As a Man Thinketh*. New York: The Science Press, 1907.

Augustine, Dennis F. *Invisible Means of Support*. Saratoga, California: Golden Gate Publishing, 1994.

Aurelius, Marcus. *Meditations of Marcus Aurelius*. 1692.

Bach, Richard. *Illusions: The Adventures of a Reluctant Messiah*. New York: Dell, 1977.

Baldwin, Christina. *Life's Companion: Journal Writing as a Spiritual Quest*. New York: Bantam Doubleday Dell, 1990.

Bejar, Heda. *Peacemaking: Day by Day*. Erie, Pennsylvania: Pax Christi, 1985.

The Bhagavad Gita. Translated by Swami Nikhilananda. New York: Ramakrishna-Vivekananda Center, 1944.

Bloy, Leon. *Letter*, November 3, 1889.

Campbell, Joseph; and Moyers, Bill. *The Power of Myth*. New York: Doubleday, 1988.

Carlyle, Thomas. *Heroes and Hero-Worship*. 1840.

Chödrön, Pema. *When Things Fall Apart*. Boston: Shambhala Publications, 1997.

Cohen, Alan. *Dare to Be Yourself*. New York: Random House, 1991.

A Course in Miracles. Mill Valley: Foundation for Inner Peace, 1975.

Csikszentmihalyi, Mihaly. *Finding Flow*. New York: HarperCollins, 1997.

DeAngelis, Barbara. "Invitation to God," in *For the Love of God*. Benjamin Shield and Richard Carlson, eds. Novato, California: New World Library, 1997.

Emerson, Ralph Waldo. *Poetry and Imagination*. 1876.

Foster, Richard J. *Prayers from the Heart*. New York: HarperCollins, 1994.

Funk, Robert; Hoover, Roy; and The Jesus Seminar. *The Five Gospels*. New York: HarperCollins, 1997.

Hanh, Thich Nhat. *For a Future to Be Possible: Commentaries on the Five Mindfulness Trainings*. Berkeley, California: Parallax Press, 1998.

————. *The Long Road Turns to Joy: A Guide to Walking Meditation*. Berkeley, California: Parallax Press, 1996.

————. *Peace is Every Step*. New York: Bantam, 1991.

————. *Teachings on Love*. Berkeley, California: Parallax Press, 1997.

Harvey, Andrew. *Dialogues With a Modern Mystic*. Wheaton, IL: Quest Books, 1994.

Heschel, Abraham Joshua. *The Wisdom of Heschel*. New York: Farrar, Straus and Giroux, Inc., 1975.

Holmes, Ernest. *Creative Mind and Success*. New York: R. M. McBride & Company, 1919.

The Holy Bible. King James Version.

The Holy Bible. Revised Standard Version.

The Holy Bible. New Oxford Annotated Bible with the Apocrypha. New York: Oxford University Press, 1973.

The Holy Bible. New Revised Standard Version, 1989.

Huxley, Aldous. *Music At Night*. New York: HarperCollins, 1931.

Keller, Helen. *Helen Keller's Journal, 1936-37*. New York: The American Foundation for the Blind.

Kornfield, Jack. *Buddha's Little Instruction Book*. New York: Bantam Books, 1994.

Le Guin, Ursula K. *The Left Hand of Darkness*. New York: Walker, 1969.

Longfellow, Henry Wadsworth. *Driftwood*. 1857.

Maggio, Rosalie. *The Beacon Book of Quotations by Women*. Boston: Beacon Press, 1992.

Peale, Norman Vincent. *A Guide to Confident Living*. New York: Fawcett Columbine, 1996.

Peter, Laurence. *Peter's Quotations*. New York: Bantam Books, 1977.

Phillips, Mike. *The Seven Laws of Money*. Boston: Shambhala Publications, 1974.

Porter, Elena H. *Pollyanna*. 1912.

Rilke, Ranier Maria. *Poems*. Translated by Jessie Lemont. New York: Columbia University Press, 1943.

Roy, Dilip Kumar. *Pilgrims of the Stars*. Timeless Books, 1985.

Salzberg, Sharon, in *Insight Newsletter*, Spring 1997. Barre, Massachusetts: Barre Center for Buddhist Studies.

————. *Lovingkindness*. Boston: Shambhala Publications, 1995.

Schiller, David. *The Little Zen Companion*. New York: Workman Publishing, 1994.

Schwartz, Richard; and Olds, Jacqueline. *Overcoming Loneliness*. Carol Publishing, 1996.

Sheen, Fulton J. *Our Sunday Visitor*. Huntington, Indiana: Our Sunday Visitor Publishing, March 11, 1962.

Shinn, Florence Scovel. *The Power of the Spoken Word*. Marina del Rey, California: DeVorss & Company, 1945.

Stoppard, Tom. *Rosencratz and Guildenstern Are Dead*. London: Faber & Faber Ltd., 1967.

Suzuki, D.T. *Zen Buddhism: Selected Writings of D.T. Suzuki*. New York: Doubleday, 1996.

St. Teresa of Avila, *The Interior Castle*. 1575.

Mother Teresa. *A Simple Path*. New York: Ballantine Books, 1995.

Thoele, Sue Patton. *A Woman's Book of Confidence*. Berkeley: Conari Press, 1992.

Walsch, Neale Donald. *Conversations with God*. New York: G.P. Putnam's Sons, 1991.

Weil, Simone. *The Need for Roots: Prelude to a Declaration of Duties Toward Mankind*. Florence, Kentucky: Routledge Inc., 1949.

Woods, Ralph. *The World Treasury of Religious Quotations*. New York: Hawthorn Books, 1966.

Yogananda, Paramahansa. *The Divine Romance*. Los Angeles: Self-Realization Fellowship, 1986.

CREDITS

Augustine, Dennis F. *Invisible Means of Support*. Copyright ©1994 by Dr. Dennis F. Augustine. Used by permission of Golden Gate Publishing.

Bach, Richard. *Illusions: The Adventures of a Reluctant Messiah*. Copyright ©1977 by Richard Bach and Leslie Parriah-Bach. Used by permission of Delacorte Press, a division of Bantam Doubleday Dell Publishing Group, Inc.

Baldwin, Christina. *Life's Companion: Journal Writing as a Spiritual Quest*. Copyright ©1990 by Christina Baldwin. Used by permission of Bantam Books, a division of Bantam Doubleday Dell Publishing Group, Inc.

Bejar, Heda. *Peacemaking: Day by Day*. Erie, Pennsylvania: Pax Christi, 1985. Reprinted by permission of Pax Christi.

Campbell, Joseph; and Moyers, Bill. *The Power of Myth*. Copyright ©1988 by Apostrophe S Productions, Inc., and Bill Moyers and Alfred van der Marck Editions, Inc. for itself and the estate of Joseph Campbell. Used by permission of Doubleday, a division of Bantam Doubleday Dell Publishing Group, Inc.

Chödrön, Pema. *When Things Fall Apart*. Copyright ©1997 by Pema Chödrön. Reprinted by arrangement with Shambhala Publications, Inc., Boston.

Cohen, Alan. *Dare to Be Yourself*. Copyright © 1991 by Alan Cohen. Reprinted by permission of Random House, Inc.

Csikszentmihalyi, Mihaly. *Finding Flow.* Copyright © 1997 by Mihaly
    Csikszentmihalyi. Reprinted by permission of BasicBooks, a subsidiary
    of Perseus Group, LLC.

DeAngelis, Barbara. "Invitation to God." Excerpted from *For the Love of God* by
    Benjamin Shield and Richard Carlson, eds. Novato, California: New
    World Library, ©1997. Reprinted with permission of New World
    Library, Novato, CA 94949.

Hahn, Thich Nhat. *For a Future to Be Possible: Commentaries on the Five Mindfulness
    Trainings.* Copyright © 1998 by Thich Nhat Hanh. Reprinted with per-
    mission of Parallax Press, Berkeley, California.

————. "The Peace of the Divine Reality." *For the Love of God* by Benjamin Shield
    and Richard Carlson, eds. Novato, California: New World Library, ©1997.
    Reprinted with permission of New World Library, Novato, California.

————. *Living Buddha, Living Christ.* Copyright © 1995 by Thich Nhat Hanh.
    Reprinted with permission of Riverhead Books, a division of Penguin
    Putnam.

————. *The Long Road Turns to Joy: A Guide to Walking Meditation.* Copyright
    © 1996 by Thich Nhat Hanh. Reprinted with permission of Parallax
    Press, Berkeley, California.

————. *Peace is Every Step.* Copyright ©1991 by Thich Nhat Hanh. Used by
    permission of Bantam Books, a division of Bantam Doubleday Dell
    Publishing Group, Inc.

————. *Teachings on Love.* Copyright © 1997 by Thich Nhat Hanh. Reprinted with permission of Parallax Press, Berkeley, California.

Harvey, Andrew. *Dialogues With a Modern Mystic.* Copyright ©1994 by Andrew Harvey and Mark Matousek. Reprinted with permission of Quest Books, Wheaton, Illinois.

Heschel, Abraham Joshua. *The Wisdom of Heschel.* Copyright © 1975 by Sylvia Heschel. Reprinted by permission of Farrar, Straus and Giroux, Inc.

Keller, Helen. *Helen Keller's Journal, 1936–37.* Courtesy of The American Foundation for the Blind, Helen Keller Archives.

Kornfield, Jack. *Buddha's Little Instruction Book.* Copyright ©1994 by Jack Kornfield. Used by permission of Bantam Books, a division of Bantam Doubleday Dell Publishing Group, Inc.

Kushner, Harold. From a conversation with Rabbi Harold Kushner. Printed with permission of Rabbi Harold Kushner.

Le Guin, Ursula K. *The Left Hand of Darkness.* Copyright © 1969 by Ursula K. Le Guin. Reprinted with permission from Walker & Co, New York.

Peale, Norman Vincent. *A Guide to Confident Living.* Copyright © 1948 by Prentice-Hall, Inc.; copyright renewed (c) 1976 by Norman Vincent Peale. Reprinted with the permission of Simon & Schuster.

Walsch, Neale Donald. *Conversations with God.* Copyright ©1995 by Neale Donald Walsch. Reprinted by permission of The Putnam Publishing Group.

Weil, Simone. *The Need for Roots: Prelude to a Declaration of Duties Toward Mankind.* Florence, Kentucky: Routledge Inc., 1949.

Yogananda, Paramahansa. Quotations from the writings of Paramahansa Yogananda published by Self-Realization Fellowship, Los Angeles. Used by permission of Self-Realization Fellowship.